Cost-based Pricing in the NHS Internal Market

Sheila Ellwood
The University of Aston in Birmingham

The Chartered Institute of Management Accountants
63 Portland Place
London W1N 4AB

First published in 1996 by:
The Chartered Institute of Management Accountants

ISBN 1 874784 41 8

The publisher of this book considers that it is a worthwhile contribution to discussion, without necessarily sharing the views expressed, which are those of the author.

No responsibility for loss occasioned to any person acting or refraining from action as a result of any material in this publication can be accepted by the author or publisher.

Contents

Dedication

To Graham and Alice – their value cannot be costed or priced.

Acknowledgements

My appreciation is extended to the directors and accountants working in the NHS who generously gave their time to assist in the case studies and the surveys.

I am also grateful to CIMA for providing funds for an earlier research project which gave the impetus for this longitudinal study of cost-based pricing in the NHS Internal Market.

Abbreviations

ABC	Activity-based costing
ALOS	Average length of stay
AYMB	Arthur Young management budgeting
BMA	British Medical Association
BUPA	British United Provident Association
CASPE	Clinical accountability service planning and evaluation
CCU	Coronary care unit
CIPFA	Chartered Institute of Public Finance and Accountancy
DGH	District general hospital
DoH	Department of Health
DHA	District health authority
DHSS	Department of Health and Social Security
DMU	Directly managed unit
DRG	Diagnosis-related group
ECR	Extra-contractual referral
EFG	Extended fundholder group
ENT	Ear, nose and throat
FCE	Finished consultant episode
FHSA	Family Health Service Authority (formerly FPC)
FIP	Financial information project
FPC	Family Practitioner Committee
FR	Financial return
GPFH	General practitioner fundholder
HFMA	Healthcare Financial Management Association
HISS	Hospital information support system
HRG	Healthcare resource group
ICD	International classification of diseases
ITU	Intensive therapy unit
LRAC	Long-run average cost
LRMC	Long-run marginal cost
MARS	Medical activity resource system
NAHAT	National Association of Health Authorities and Trusts
NEMC	New England Medical Center
NHSME	National Health Service Management Executive
NSGC	National Steering Group on Costing

PTS	Patient treatment services
RCC	Ratio of costs to charges
RHA	Regional health authority
RM	Resource management
RVU	Relative value unit
SAPPS	Specialty and procedure pricing system
SCBU	Special care baby unit
TFR	Trust financial return
WMRHA	West Midlands Regional Health Authority

Glossary

Acute services

A range of health services, usually provided in a hospital setting, for people with diagnosed acute illness.

Block contract

A contract between a purchaser of health services and a provider of health services, which gives access to a defined range of services for an annual fee paid in instalments.

Capital charges

An amount equivalent to depreciation and 6 per cent interest on fixed assets, included in prices charged by directly managed hospitals, and payable by district health authorities to regional health authorities.

Case mix

Frequency of patients falling into types according to some pre-determined characteristics. These may be social, demographic or severity measures, but are more normally diagnosis, age and treatment. The number of cases in each group can be used to calculate a case-mix index.

Clinical accountability, service planning and evaluation

The CASPE Research Unit pioneered the involvement of clinicians (sometimes with nursing and other disciplines) in financial planning and budgeting projects, notably through the system of planning agreements with clinical teams (PACTs).

Clinical directorate

Sub-hospital organisation structure, based on a defined group of patient services, such as general surgery or pathology, that is devolved responsibility for its own activities. It is multi-disciplinary, and managed by a director who is usually a clinician.

Cost and volume contract

A contract between a purchaser and a provider under which payment is made for a set level of service, usually expressed as a maximum number of cases, treatments or interventions. Once the agreed maximum is reached, additional payment is made on the basis of individual cases within an overall limit.

Coefficient of variation (CV)

The ratio of the standard deviation to the mean, used as a measure of dispersion. It is sometimes considered that a coefficient of variation should be less than 1 for a homogeneous distribution.

Day-case surgery

An operation for which the patient is admitted and discharged on the same day.

Diagnosis-related group (DRG)

Groupings of patients that are clinically and resource homogeneous as defined by the developers of the scheme at Yale School of Management. Each case belongs to one and only one of some 500 groups. It can be assigned after inspecting the principal diagnosis, main operation, secondary diagnosis, age, sex and discharge disposition from a patient computer abstract.

Elective surgery

Surgical treatment for patients which is planned or booked, i.e. not an emergency.

Finished consultant episode (FCE)

A period of care in which a patient is registered under a consultant, applied to in-patient and day cases.

Healthcare Resource Group (HRG)

Groupings of patients developed by the National Case Mix Office which are clinically similar (homogeneous) and can be expected to consume similar amounts of resource (iso-resource).

Medicare

The US publicly funded and administered health insurance scheme which covers people over 65 years old and the disabled, irrespective of income levels.

Medical audit

The NHS reforms obliged all doctors to examine the quality of their care collectively with other members of their specialty, clinical group or practice. Managers must be informed of results and can initiate specific audits.

Resource management (RM) database

The principal database management system implemented by RM hospitals. A centralised database designed to support planning, monitoring and evaluation of patient services.

Specialty division

A grouping together of medical staff in related areas of work.

Executive Summary

In 1991, the NHS internal market was introduced – the most dramatic change in the organisation of the NHS since its inception. The price mechanism is crucial to the efficient operation of the market. The NHS Management Executive (NHSME) imposed a full-cost pricing regime. This research study addresses whether cost-based pricing can be employed to facilitate economic efficiency in the NHS internal market. Following a review of markets and healthcare cost accounting, the study encompasses surveys of NHS acute healthcare providers in 1991 and 1994 and two case studies.

In the first year of the market, it was evident that cost-based prices were not feeding appropriate signals to purchasers. The prices were not based on accurate, reliable costs: poor methods of cost attribution were adopted. Contracts were largely placed at specialty level which provided an imprecise definition of services (products) – variations in case mix within specialties were not addressed. On the other hand, where procedure prices were compiled (namely for GP fundholders) they were often based on inadequate data and cost methods. Thus prices were not reliable indicators of resources consumed. Efficiency comparisons between providers were not possible: price differences may have been spurious owing to inadequate methods and a lack of consistency in cost allocation and apportionment methods between different hospitals.

The 1994 survey showed that cost methods have developed and, following detailed guidance from the NHSME, consistency has improved, but a lack of activity information remains. Price variations due to costing approaches rather than differing resource use still persist. The thorny problem of adequately defining the healthcare products for costing purposes remains to be resolved. Attempts are being made to use healthcare resource groups (HRGs) for this purpose.

The wider issues surrounding costing for healthcare contracting were examined through the case studies. The case studies of the costing process at two acute service providers enabled the factors influencing the cost methods to be examined. Conflict between the requirement for a uniform approach to costing and the financial management needs at local level was apparent. Even more illuminating were the pricing and contract negotiation stages which superseded the costing process. Evidence of extensive cost-shifting and price manipulation was found. Published prices are a starting point: the overall contract value is subject to negotiation, and the providers inevitably have long-term relationships with their purchasers. The emerging internal market is a set of oligopolies and oligopsonies in which inter-organisational bargaining is the central mechanism by which resources are allocated. Such an environment is incompatible with the simulation of the pricing regime of the perfectly competitive market. Financial management and market incentives encourage the manipulation of full-cost prices and, given the make-up of healthcare costs, this can be achieved relatively easily. In the search for a new policy paradigm to replace the traditional, top-down planning model, cost-based pricing within an internal market cannot be used to ensure a more efficient use of NHS resources. If the quasi-market is to be efficiency driven, either measures must be taken to refine, monitor and enforce cost-based pricing rules, or other ways of managing the market must be considered.

1 Introduction

1.1 Background

Since 1988, a programme of market-oriented change has been introduced into the UK welfare state. The extent and speed of the introduction of 'market forces' into the welfare state was dramatic and has been referred to as the 'big bang' (*Le Grand,* 1994). In 1988 the Griffiths Report on personal social services *(Griffiths,* 1988) was published: care managers at a local level were to become budget holders and purchase the best package of care for individual clients from a wider variety of competing agencies. That year also saw the setting up of a comprehensive review into the NHS, a review that culmi-nated in the 1989 White Paper, *Working for Patients* (*Department of Health,* 1989a).

The health service reforms embodied in the 1990 NHS and Community Care Act and introduced on 1 April 1991 represent the greatest change in the organisation and management of the NHS since it was established in 1948. In essence, an internal market has been created within the NHS in which district health authorities (DHAs) and general practice fundholders (GPFHs) have responsibility for commissioning or purchasing services; and directly managed units (DMUs) and NHS trusts have the responsibility for providing them.

All these developments thus involve the introduction of quasi-markets into the welfare state. 'They are "markets" because they replace monolithic state providers [within a top-down planning model] with competitive independent ones. They are "quasi" because they differ from conventional markets in a number of key ways' (*Le Grand and Bartlett,* 1993). In contrast to conventional markets, competitive providers (schools, universities, residential homes, hospitals) are not necessarily out to maximise their profits nor are they necessarily privately owned. On the demand side, purchasers are often not the consumers of services and receive their funding from the public purse according to some prescribed formulae.

The introduction of competition is supposed to encourage a more economical use of resources, thus improving technical efficiency. More importantly, the introduction of competing suppliers could improve allocative efficiency. Welfare users, or at least their agents, should have alternative sources of supply. However, there is very little research concerning how markets for publicly funded services should operate to stimulate the desired efficiency gains. This research study examines the role of cost accounting in pricing healthcare under the NHS internal market or 'managed competition'. The study covers hospital provision of acute health services; long-stay services for the elderly and the mentally ill are excluded.

1.2 Research methods

The use of price signals to distribute resources within the welfare state is a new social policy paradigm. The feasibility of such an approach in healthcare provision was largely untested at the introduction of the NHS internal market. The NHS reforms have no obvious parallel in healthcare systems abroad, nor was there significant pilot testing in the UK prior to their introduction on 1 April 1991. This research study considers whether cost-based pricing can provide appropriate signals to facilitate a more efficient use of NHS financial resources.

Assessing the validity of cost-based price signals requires two issues to be examined in depth: the development of cost-based prices which are reasonable measures of resource consumption (homogeneous product groupings with realistic methods of cost attribution); and comparable prices of alternative providers (consistency in terms of cost products and methods of cost attribution). Furthermore, in order for the desired improvements in economic efficiency to be realised, purchasers must act on the price signals; and providers should be encouraged to strive for efficiency through competition and/or openness in costing. The research framework is illustrated in Figure 1.1.

Figure 1.1: The research framework

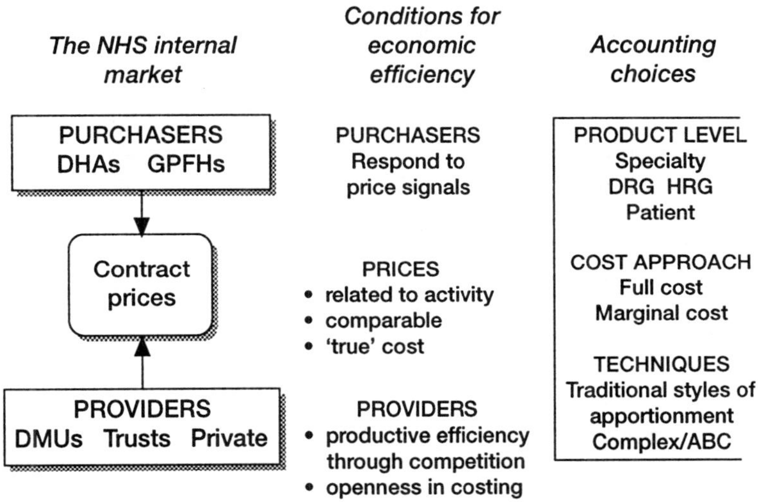

To evaluate the cost-based prices, information on cost accounting approaches adopted in compiling contract prices in the NHS internal market had to be collected. Surveys could be used to gather a large volume of data on the development of NHS costing for pricing. However, a major limitation is frequently evident – the inability to explain *why*. Case studies are becoming increasingly popular in accounting research. A case study is a single unit of analysis which offers depth or richness of detail and therefore the possibility of understanding the nature of accounting in practice. This understanding can be in terms of the accounting techniques, procedures, systems, etc., which are used and the way in which they are used. As such they are useful in attempting to determine the gap between accounting theory and practice. It has long been accepted that the conventional wisdom of management accounting textbooks is not widely used in practice (*Ryan et al.*, 1992). In the context of this research study, it is quite possible that there may be differences between NHS guidance and regulations concerning cost-based pricing and practice. Mohr in his defence of the case study *(Mohr*, 1985) points out that 'external validity (generalisation) can hardly be a legitimate issue until internal validity ... the truth of the statement made about the subjects and events that are actually observed ... is positively settled.'

The particular approach adopted in this research study was a combination of survey and case study methods. This would not only maximise the amount of data collected, but would allow the advantages of alternative methods to be gained while alleviating some potential flaws incurred when concentrating solely on one method.

A preliminary review of healthcare cost accounting provided an initial indication of the problems and potential for cost accounting methods in pricing healthcare. Following the review, surveys were used to enable the cost-based pricing methods used by many hospitals in the NHS to be identified and described economically. By undertaking two surveys (one at the commencement of the internal market and a follow-up survey three years later), we can describe how cost-based pricing has progressed as the NHS internal market has matured. However, in order to provide the richness of detail and a fuller understanding of the issues surrounding the process in NHS hospitals, case studies were needed.

The West Midlands Health Region was chosen as the area of the surveys. The West Midlands Region covers approximately 10 per cent of the NHS in England (expressed in either cost or population); it has a cross-section of urban and rural areas and a range of acute hospitals from major teaching hospitals to small town district general hospitals. These are listed in Table 1.1.

Table 1.1: Acute hospitals in the West Midlands region 1991

District Health Authority	Hospital
Bromsgrove and Redditch	Alexandra
	Highfield
Herefordshire	Hereford County
	Hereford General
	The Victoria Eye
Kidderminster and District	Bewdley Road
	Tenbury Wells
Worcester and District	Worcester Royal Infirmary
	Evesham General
Shropshire	Princess Royal
	Robert Jones & Agnes Hunt
	Royal Shrewsbury
	Ear Eye and Throat

Continued...

Mid Staffordshire	Stafford
	The General Infirmary
North Staffordshire	The Royal Infirmary
	The City General
SE Staffordshire	Burton DHC
	Burton General
	Tamworth General
Rugby	St Cross
North Warwickshire	George Eliot
	The Manor
Central Birmingham	Queen Elizabeth
	Birmingham Women's
	Birmingham General
	Birmingham Children's
East Birmingham	East Birmingham
North Birmingham	Good Hope
	Highcroft
South Birmingham	Selly Oak
	Royal Orthopaedic
West Birmingham	Dudley Road
	Birmingham Eye & Skin
Coventry	Walsgrave
	Coventry and Warwick
	Paybody
Dudley	Wordsley
	Corbett
	Russells Hall and Guest
Sandwell	Sandwell DG
Solihull	Solihull
	Marston Green
Walsall	Manor
Wolverhampton	New Cross
	The Royal
	Eye Infirmary
South Warwickshire	Stratford
	Warneford

The surveys included a price database of treatment prices for all NHS acute healthcare providers in the West Midlands Health Region and questionnaires on the approaches adopted in costing and pricing healthcare. A more detailed picture of the research issues was gained from the case studies. Two case studies (the St Somewhere NHS Trust and the Thereabouts Acute Unit) were chosen from different geographic environments, with large variations in terms of size and complexity of service provision.

1.3 The structure of the report

The first four chapters cover the theory of healthcare markets, pricing and cost determination. Chapter 2 examines markets and healthcare from an economic perspective. The nature of markets and their perceived operation is identified before depicting the NHS internal market. Alternative forms of governance structure and their relevance to healthcare are then briefly considered. Chapter 3 examines the incentives and scope for economic efficiency in the NHS internal market. The internal market model, it is argued, requires price signals which indicate the comparative efficiency of healthcare providers. Healthcare pricing theory and experience are considered in the light of the prescribed cost-based pricing regime set out for the NHS internal market. Chapter 4 examines accounting information for pricing decisions. Appropriate cost 'products' are discussed before examining different methods of attributing hospital costs.

Chapter 5 provides a review of cost accounting information in healthcare prior to the introduction of the NHS internal market. Information available nationally and under specific initiatives in the UK is set out, followed by consideration of how healthcare is costed in the USA where a market approach to healthcare has been adopted.

Chapters 6 to 10 contain empirical research on healthcare cost accounting and pricing. Chapters 6 and 7 cover the two surveys of hospitals in the West Midlands Health Region. The initial survey (Chapter 6) was undertaken in 1991 to show the cost methods adopted in deriving the prices for healthcare contracts in the first year of the market. In 1994, a further survey of hospitals in the West Midlands (Chapter 7) was undertaken to show how costing for contracting has developed following subsequent guidance from the NHS Management Executive (NHSME). Chapter 8 sets out case studies of the costing for pricing process at two acute healthcare providers. The costing and pricing processes prior to and following the detailed NHSME guidance are examined. Price comparability and accounting choices are discussed in Chapter 9. Chapter 10 examines how the acute healthcare providers negotiated their 1994/95 healthcare contracts. The case studies provide an in-depth analysis of costing and pricing while including a wider perspective of the issues surrounding the contracting process. The nature of the NHS internal market is considered in the context of the NHS pricing regime.

Chapter 11 considers the implications of the research study for the future development of cost-based pricing in the NHS, and draws conclusions.

2

Markets and Healthcare: An Economic Perspective

2.1 Introduction

This chapter identifies the nature of markets and their perceived operation before depicting the NHS internal market. Alternative forms of governance structure (hierarchies, networks and clans) are briefly considered and their relevance to the NHS discussed.

2.2 Markets

A market is basically an adjustment mechanism for supply and demand which enables the exchange of goods and services between consumers and producers. The perceived operation of markets varies according to the market conditions underlying the analysis and the school of thought.

Market conditions

Market conditions can range from perfect competition at one extreme (with lots of buyers and sellers, and no one agent powerful enough to determine price levels) to monopoly at the other.

Monopolistic or oligopolistic competition is a midway position in which a number of competitive enterprises are large enough to have at least some control, though not total control, over the market price.

Schools of economic thought

Neo-classical

The dominant idea of neo-classical economics is of a series of separate firms maximising their profits via adapting their outputs to the given ruling price. Prices act as the crucial equilibrating mechanism between producers and consumers. Decision-makers, already in possession of the required information about market conditions and the ruling price, adjust their behaviour to reach a 'static' equilibrium position where no one can be made better off without at least one person being made worse off.

Neo-Austrian

In the Neo-Austrian or 'competitive process' approach, the market is seen as a process of selection, turmoil and change where conditions of disequilibrium prevail. Less emphasis is put on price and more on the (beneficial) effects of the competitive process that the market engenders. Competition and entrepreneurship are regarded as important aspects of the market process which are largely ignored in neo-classical economics. Many decisions which are carried out may not turn out to be the best possible course of action. The market process is set in motion by the results of initial market ignorance of the participants. Competition between consumers for each commodity may tend to force its price upwards; competition among owners of a particular resource may tend to force its price downwards. This school of thought is enhanced by contestable market theory.

Contestable market theory

A contestable market is one in which the positions of incumbents are easily contested by entrants.

Under these circumstances, *Baumol et al.* (1988) argue that a perfectly contestable market offers many of the benefits hereto associated only with perfect competition. They see monopolists and oligopolists who populate such markets as 'sheep in wolves' clothing', because in perfectly contestable markets rivals can be as effective as actual competitors in forcing efficient behaviour. Entrepreneurs are assumed to be profit-seekers who take advantage of all profitable opportunities for entry. Potential entrants assess the profitability of their marketing plans by making use of the current prices of incumbent firms.

Baumol et al. argue that, in a contestable market, firms must operate efficiently in order to survive. If a firm were to earn profits while producing at costs greater than necessary, an entrant could undercut the firm's prices and earn a positive profit by operating more efficiently. Similarly, an incumbent firm is forced to adopt any new techniques capable of reducing costs, for failure to do so will invite entry by firms that do employ cost-saving innovations. Cross-subsidies cannot be sustained: if any set of products of the incumbent firms does not yield incremental net revenues as great as its incremental net costs, then an entrant can cut prices and nevertheless earn more than the incumbent previously did (e.g. by offering only the remunerative products). Moreover, total industry output must be distributed among firms in a way that minimises total industry cost. If some rearrangement of output among firms could reduce total cost, then an entrant whose size was consistent with that rearrangement could earn a profit at prices below that previously held (assuming frictionless free entry). The implication of the above propositions for the case of monopoly is that, in a contestable market, a monopoly cannot persist unless it is the least costly provider of its array of outputs.

Thus markets operate quite differently according to the conditions underlying the analysis; furthermore, different schools of thought perceive them to operate in deviating ways. For example, monopoly, for the neo-classical school, is a highly undesirable state of affairs that undermines all the advantages of the competitive market. It can lead to exploitation of the monopolist's power in the market so that prices are fixed above their economically efficient level and excess profits are earned by the monopolist. Monopolists therefore need to be closely monitored by the public authorities and dismantled by government action as and when they abuse their dominant market position. However, for the neo-Austrian school, monopoly may simply be the result of past successful entrepreneurial initiative and dynamic competitive activity. Firms need to be allowed to capture monopoly rents that research and development investment and advertising capital produce if society is to reap the full benefits that dynamic competition fosters. They argue that the 'social costs' of monopoly profits and disequilibrium prices may be exaggerated and anyway these will be transitory and short run as they are bid away by the operation of the market – as long as the market is contestable, monopoly profits cannot be sustained in the long term.

A further divergence is the profit maximisation objective. In neo-classical economics profit maximisation is seen as the means by which a firm survives and prospers. On the other hand, in the competitive process approach, the problem for the firm is to continue and prosper in the face of continual threat of new entrants to the market. Price provides the basis for the income of the firm which, relative to its costs, determines the firm's profits and investment strategies.

Within the schools of thought, consumer sovereignty holds the supreme advantage that it allows consumers to choose independently how they will deploy their spending power, and in turn this will lead to the correct allocation of resources to meet those consumer needs. Prices produce a signalling device that contributes spontaneously and voluntarily to an efficient and prosperous co-existence of all elements in the social process.

2.3 Healthcare markets

Although no markets work perfectly (according to the neo-classical ideal situation outlined earlier), leaving the resource allocation process to be determined by market forces may still remain the best way of getting as close as possible to the outcomes of the perfectly competitive market. Many imperfect markets are highly competitive and therefore the 'competitive process' may be of benefit to consumers. Further, it has been argued that as long as markets are contestable, firms must operate efficiently. However, healthcare is characterised by extensive government intervention in most developed countries, as shown in Table 2.1.

Economics and healthcare

The basic reasoning for government intervention is that none of the ideal assumptions of perfectly competitive markets work in the case of healthcare (*Donaldson and Gerard*, 1993). They argue that market failure in the allocation of healthcare is so complete that extensive government intervention is more likely to result in the achievement of societal objectives than are market forces supplemented by minimal government intervention.

In healthcare markets a number of factors impede efficient market operation.

Table 2.1: Government intervention in healthcare: selected international comparisons

Country	% of healthcare government funded (1987)
Australia	84.5
Austria	60.9
Belgium	91.6
Canada	74.4
Denmark	83.4
Finland	78.8
France	71.2
Germany	78.2
Greece	79.3
Ireland	86.9
Italy	84.1
Japan	72.1
Netherlands	78.3
New Zealand	78.4
Norway	88.8
Portugal	71.1
Spain	72.3
Sweden	91.4
UK	88.9
USA	41.4

Source: *OECD* (1989)

Uncertainty

Uncertainty surrounds the consumption of many items of healthcare; deteriorations in health are often sudden or unexpected. In addition, the healthcare required to offset such health problems may be expensive and unaffordable. Health insurance markets may develop to counter the financial burdens of ill health. Such markets experience some problems similar to those encountered with publicly financed health services, as well as others such as moral hazard and adverse selection which give rise to the need for government regulation.

Consumer moral hazard is a change in the attitudes of consumers of healthcare which results from being insured against the full costs of such care. Zero or reduced price at the point of use encourages a higher rate of use than would otherwise be considered efficient. Provider moral hazard can arise from a simple lack of awareness or from the use of fee-for-service remuneration methods for doctors in which fees depart from 'market prices'.

Adverse selection results from asymmetry of information in the insurance market whereby the best risks are selected out of the insured group. A consequence of adverse selection is that people may be left uninsured. Moral hazard and adverse selection in healthcare markets are discussed further by *Donaldson and Gerard* (1993).

Externalities

Externalities are spillovers from other people's production or consumption of commodities which affect the individual in either a negative or positive way, but which are out of the individual's control. The costs and benefits of such spillovers cannot be accounted for in market transactions, because when such transactions take place consumers and suppliers consider only costs and benefits to themselves.

The reliance of the market on self-interest leads to a misallocation of resources when externalities exist: oversupply when negative externalities exist and undersupply when positive externalities exist. An obvious form of positive externality in healthcare is the benefit to one's own health from other people's vaccinations. Further positive externalities may arise from knowing that someone else is receiving needed healthcare even if this does not impact on one's own health status.

Imperfect knowledge

The consumer of healthcare is often unaware of his health status and all the options available to contribute to an improvement in health; he has imperfect knowledge of the technological relationship between healthcare and health improvements or health maintenance. For many common ailments and some chronic conditions the consumer may be aware of his health status and the treatment options available, but this is unlikely to be the case for more acute conditions such as cancers. Even in the case of minor or chronic ailments, information on new developments in treatment may get through to healthcare providers long before it reaches the consumer.

The accumulation of knowledge is also determined by the regularity with which one uses the market. Much medical care is not repeated, so that even if a consumer finds out that a treatment was not suitable, it will in many cases be too late to change to another. In other words, neither before nor after treatment can consumers easily acquire information to make an informed choice.

Consumers are unable to act free of self-interested advice from suppliers

As explained above, suppliers act in their own interest to provide commodities most highly valued by consumers relative to their prices. Given the lack of perfect knowledge on the part of the consumers of healthcare, doctors are often placed in the position of providing expert advice to consumers about care to be provided by themselves or their colleagues. Thus the supplier of healthcare is able to influence substantially the demand for healthcare. Moreover, there may be situations in which doctors have a financial incentive to provide care of no value or little value relative to its cost.

Monopolistic suppliers

The existence of the information imbalance confers considerable monopoly power on the suppliers of medical services. As patients find it difficult to 'shop around' intelligently, it is less likely that doctors and hospitals will compete with one another. Each can operate as a monopoly raising prices and perhaps offering a lower quality of service without fearing a substantial loss of customers. As *Le Grand and Robinson* (1984) conclude:

> *'This is not to imply that all doctors act as rapacious exploiters out to extract as much profit as possible from their patients. Rather it is simply acknowledging that many of the incentives for efficiency normally present in a competitive market are conspicuously absent in that for healthcare.'*

Market failure and healthcare is examined further in a number of texts: *Le Grand and Robinson* (1984), *McGuire et al.* (1988), *Donaldson and Gerard* (1993).

Equity and access to healthcare are also problems resulting from a market allocation of healthcare. There are three conceptions of equity commonly used in a healthcare context (*Le Grand and Robinson*, 1984): a minimum standard of treatment for all in need; equal treatment for equal need; and equality of access or cost. In a private market, poor people may not be able to purchase the treatment they need – there is no guarantee that everyone will be able to obtain at least a minimum level of healthcare. Those with higher incomes are likely to purchase better treatment and consequently there will be unequal treatment for equal need. The price of healthcare would represent a greater sacrifice for the poor than for the better off and therefore inequality of access would persist.

Healthcare systems in practice – an international context

There are essentially only four ways of financing healthcare:

- direct payment by users;
- private health insurance;
- social or state insurance;
- direct tax.

Within each method there are many variants, and there are many possible combinations of basic methods (and their variants) within one healthcare system (Figure 2.1). Healthcare in the UK is predominantly financed by direct tax, but has some direct payment by users (which has increased markedly in recent years) and a level of private insurance. The German and French healthcare systems tend towards social insurance. In the USA, the healthcare economy is dominated by private insurance whilst in Sweden financing is more like that of the UK.

Figure 2.1: Alternatives for healthcare financing

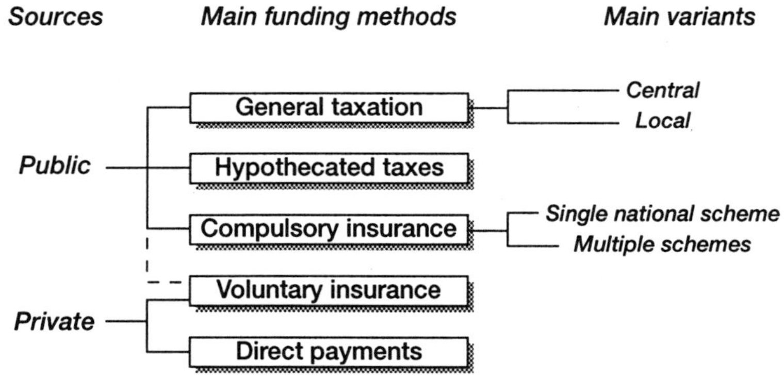

Source: *Maxwell* (1988)

All methods of funding have their weaknesses. Tax funding has many advantages, not least in enabling expenditure to be controlled, promoting equity and access, and allowing services to be provided to the whole population, but in the UK it has failed to deliver the volume of services demanded by the public (*Jowell et al.*, 1988).

Social insurance offers a middle way between tax financing and private insurance. Social insurance is an earmarked tax levied on a narrower tax base than general taxation. Individuals are able to see that their contribution is spent on health services, contributions can be increased or controlled in response to public pressure, and in some countries (e.g. Germany) certain people can opt out of the state scheme if they prefer to make their own arrangements. It is also possible to ensure that the costs of catastrophic illness will be met and that those out of work or on low incomes have coverage. However, increases in insurance contributions have been a cause for concern particularly when these have been used to finance a system of healthcare in which there is evidence of inefficiency and over-provision. Social insurance is also a more regressive form of funding than general taxation, and inequities can arise if social insurance is administered through sick funds setting different contribution rates.

The USA has the highest percentage of private financing (33 per cent direct payments and 28 per cent from insurance premiums (*Appleby*, 1992)); over 37 million people are uninsured. Systems which rely on private finance have considerable difficulty in controlling overall expenditure and severe problems in achieving equitable access to services. These disadvantages are so great that *Ham et al.* (1990) conclude:

> *'The US experience demonstrates the shortcomings of systems that rely mainly on private insurance, and indicates that the real choice facing policy makers is between social insurance and tax funding.'*

As regards the overall level of healthcare expenditure there is again considerable variation between countries (Table 2.2). It would appear that the overall level of spending on healthcare is much less important than the way in which the expenditure is distributed and healthcare delivered. Governments have attempted to tackle these problems through competition policy in some countries and regulation in others. A number of countries have experience of competition or have recently introduced competition into healthcare provision.

Table 2.2: Life expectancy and expenditure on health: selected international comparisons

Country	Life expectancy at birth 1992	Pop'n 1992 (m)	Real GDP per head 1991 ($)	Total spending on health (% GDP)	Spending per head on health 1991 ($)
Japan	78.6	124.5	19,390	6.8	1,771
Sweden	77.7	8.6	17,490	8.8	2,372
Spain	77.4	39.1	12,670	6.5	877
Greece	77.3	10.2	7,680	4.8	274
Canada	77.2	27.4	19,320	9.9	1,847
Netherlands	77.2	15.2	16,820	8.7	1,664
Australia	76.7	17.6	16,680	8.6	1,466
France	76.6	57.1	18,430	9.1	1,912
Israel	76.2	5.1	13,460	4.2	509
UK	75.8	57.7	16,340	6.6	1,003
Germany	75.6	80.2	19,770	9.0	1,782
USA	75.6	255.2	22,330	13.3	2,932
Ireland	75.0	3.5	11,430	8.0	886

Source: *New York Times* as reprinted in *The Independent*, 28 September 1994

In the USA, competition was promoted throughout the 1980s as a mechanism for containing costs. Cost-sharing arrangements were extended to make consumers more aware of the real costs of their healthcare. Anti-trust legislation was employed to remove various restraints on trade, thus permitting greater competition between healthcare providers. Most important of all, various managed care schemes, e.g. health maintenance organisations (HMOs) and preferred provider organisations (PPOs), grew up in competition with traditional insurance and fee-for-service providers. However, it was found necessary to supplement competitive mechanisms with regulatory instruments such as the prospective payments system. The Dekker reforms in Holland sought to introduce a market-oriented approach into a social insurance system; selective contracting by purchasers was to be encouraged, and consumers were to be enabled to choose between competing insurers. In Sweden, some county councils have contracted out health centres to private providers, and initiatives have been taken to introduce competition into public health services by giving consumers the choice of particular service providers and rewarding providers who are successful in attracting patients.

Although according to neo-classical economics healthcare cannot be allocated efficiently in an unregulated market system, neo-Austrian economic theorists and advocates of contestable markets would argue that competition, managed appropriately, could be an important stimulus to improved efficiency. Internationally, healthcare is predominantly financed through taxation or social insurance and largely provided in the public sector. However, outside the UK, there are recent initiatives relating to competition in healthcare. The development of internal markets for publicly financed health services in the UK is considered below.

2.4 The NHS internal market

Internal markets

Internal markets are not markets as the term is generally understood. They have not evolved naturally from existing factors of supply and demand; they are markets created by a business or organisation which redefines the nature of supply and demand and establishes a new relationship between consumers and providers. The organisation can, through its initial definition of market parameters, act as a powerful regulator, imposing either operating restrictions or financial controls to dictate the nature of the market.

The idea that market relationships can be used within organisations to improve communication flows and efficiency is not unique to the public sector. Writers focusing on the marketing of services, such as *Berry* (1981) and *Bateson* (1985), suggest that market relationships can be used to improve the efficiency and productivity of employees, the actual 'service providers' of service firms. *Fisk and Freshley* (1981) suggested that market relationships could improve efficiency and communications between departments within an organisation, as in the case of a clinical laboratory and other departments within a hospital. Market relationships have also been applied to industrial purchasing procedures, particularly in large vertically integrated companies in sectors such as electronics.

In the public sector the term internal or quasi-markets has been used in relation to recent government reforms to introduce competition into publicly funded services. In 1988, the welfare state was the biggest area of non-market activity in the British economy, consuming almost a quarter of the gross domestic product. However, all this was to change in the late 80s when the Government introduced a series of radical reforms in key parts of the welfare state.

Despite the breadth and diversity of the sectors involved, the reforms had a number of common features. In general, bureaucratic mechanisms of service delivery were replaced by competitive systems based on internal markets. In many of the reforms, in addition to decentralisation of decision-making, competition in provision was to be introduced. State financing of the services was to be retained, but the state was to become primarily only a purchaser of welfare services, with direct state provision replaced by a system of independent provider organisations including not-for-profit organisations, private companies and state-owned units under devolved management, competing with one another in internal or 'quasi'-markets.

> *'They are 'markets' because they replace monopolistic state providers with competitive independent ones. They are 'quasi' because they differ from conventional markets in a number of key ways ... non-profit organisations competing for public contracts, sometimes in competition with for-profit organisations; consumer purchasing power either centralised in a single purchasing agency or allocated to users in the form of vouchers rather than cash; and, in some cases, the consumers represented in the market by agents instead of operating by themselves.'*
>
> *Le Grand and Bartlett* (1993).

Quasi-markets now apply in education, healthcare, social care and housing. On the supply side, there are independent institutions (locally managed schools, universities, hospital trusts, residential homes, housing associations, private landlords) competing for customers. Yet, in contrast to conventional markets, these organisations are not profit-making or necessarily privately owned. On the demand side, consumer purchasing power takes the form of an earmarked budget for the purchase of specific services allocated to users, or centralised in a purchasing agency. In most cases it is not the direct user who exercises the choices concerning purchasing decisions. Such choices are assigned to a third party, such as a social services department or care manager in community care, or, as explained below, a GP or health authority in health care.

Propper et al. (1994) see the aim of the quasi-market reforms as being to overcome the perceived defects of the bureaucratic organisation of the welfare state, particularly in the areas of efficiency, choice and responsiveness. However, there is concern that market failure and equity or access considerations will be major problems in these welfare quasi-markets.

The NHS market reforms

In the 1989 White Paper an internal market for the NHS was seen as a mechanism for improved efficiency.

> *'The reforms ... will enable a higher quality of patient care to be obtained from the resources which the nation is able to devote to the NHS.... Over time, any extra costs should be offset by the improved efficiency which will stem from them.'* *Department of Health* (1989a)

In the internal market, district health authorities (DHAs) contract with hospitals to provide specified services in return for agreed funding. To facilitate competition between hospitals, the government introduced a number of self-governing trusts (*Department of Health*, 1989b). By April 1994, 95 per cent of hospital and community health services was provided by trusts (*Robinson and Le Grand*, 1994). Although still part of the NHS, these hospitals are free from control by DHAs and operate as self-standing business units. Trust hospitals and directly managed hospitals under the internal market earn their revenue according to the services they supply. Previously, the national NHS budget was allocated to regional health authorities which then allocated funds to district health authorities which in turn allocated a global budget to the individual hospitals/units they managed. The White Paper explained the new arrangements as follows:

> *'In future, each DHA's duty will be to buy the best service it can from its own hospitals, from other authorities' hospitals, from self-governing hospitals or from the private health sector. Hospitals for their part will have to satisfy districts that they are delivering the best and most efficient service. They will be free to offer their services to other district health authorities.'* *Department of Health* (1989a)

Contract funding brings about an effective separation of health authority functions: the responsibility for ensuring that the health needs of the population are met (i.e. the commissioning role) and the management of supply. While existing district health authorities are the main purchasers, at least in the short run, large general practitioner (GP) practices have the opportunity to become budget holders to purchase selected hospital services (*DoH*,1989d). Similarly to DHA purchasers, the GP fundholder contracts with providers of healthcare for their services on behalf of the practice's patients. GP fundholders (GPFHs) have grown unexpectedly and by April 1993 covered one in four of the population (*DoH Management Executive*, 1993). The Government described three forms of contract *(DoH*, 1989c): block contracts; cost and volume contracts; and cost per case contracts.

- *Block contracts* relate to funding a level of capacity.
- *Cost and volume contracts* specify a base-line level of activity.
- Beyond that level, funding is on a *cost per case* basis. In addition, hospitals will sometimes undertake extra-contractual referrals (ECRs). These may arise, for example, when a GP refers a patient to a hospital where the DHA within which the patient resides has not negotiated a contract, or perhaps the patient is admitted as an emergency (e.g. from a motor accident) to a hospital where the DHA has no contract.

> *'Hospitals need to keep their costs, including capital and other overheads, within the income they earn from contracts, and will accordingly need to aim for realistic pricing policies.... The development of the contract system will require improved management information both for pricing and for control (including monitoring performance as well as financial control).'* *Department of Health* (1989c)

The Department of Health's approach on the pricing of contracts was set out by the NHS Management Executive in October 1990.

- Contracts should generally be priced at cost.
- All costs including depreciation at current cost and 6 per cent interest on capital assets should be included.
- There should be no planned cross-subsidisation.

While providers were given a large degree of discretion in the detailed application of the principles, the requirement for the documentation of the pricing process for audit purposes was stressed (*NHS Management Executive*, 1990d). The assumed volume of service over which full costs should be recovered should include all expected activity in the year, including anticipated extra-contractual referrals

(ECRs). Marginal cost contracts are only permissible where there is unplanned spare capacity in excess of the assumed volume of service. The net costs to be recovered through income from services should take account of planned cost improvements.

Figure 2.2: The NHS internal market – flow of funds and services

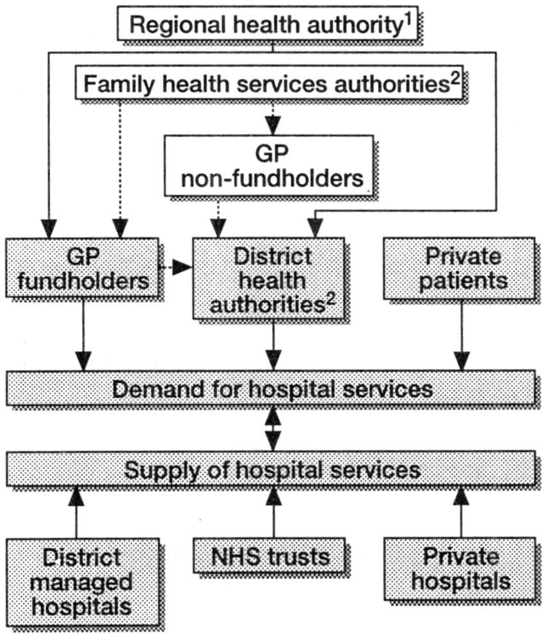

Reflect 'non GP budget' services only

1 The 14 regional health authorities were transformed into 8 regional offices of the NHS Executive on 1 April 1996

2 District health authorities and family health services authorities merged to become Health Commissions on 1 April 1996

The internal market shown in Figure 2.2 meets Le Grand and Bartlett's definition of a quasi-market (see p. 20). The healthcare providers, namely NHS trusts, directly managed units and independent hospitals, compete for healthcare contracts, replacing the centrally planned monopolistic provision. On the demand side, the consumer purchasing power is represented by agents, district health authorities and GP fundholders. Common problems associated with healthcare markets generally are alleviated in the NHS internal market. DHAs and GPFHs, acting as agents for patients, can reduce some problems relating to imperfect knowledge and monopolistic suppliers, but other problems remain. The introduction of GP fundholding provides scope for adverse selection or 'cream-skimming' (*Matsaganis and Glennerster*, 1994). DHAs have no opportunity to cream-skim as their clients are simply allotted to the DHA. However, GPFHs can compete for the custom of patients on whose behalf they purchase services, and thus there may be an incentive, in certain circumstances, for the GPFH to cream-skim (*Weiner and Ferris*, 1990) – although, as yet, there appears little evidence of this actually happening in the UK (*Glennerster et al.*, 1992).

2.5 Alternative governance structures

The transaction costs approach

The existence of the pre-reform NHS (and other large producer organisations) can be explained not only by market failure and equity and access considerations, but also by transaction costs.

> *'A transaction cost is any activity which is engaged in to satisfy each party to an exchange that the value given and received is in accord with his or her expectations.'* *Ouchi* (1993)

Coase (1937) pointed out that where transaction costs are sufficiently important, the market (as a system of resource allocation) can logically be set aside, and transactions internalised within firms or organisations.

Williamson (1971) pursued Coase's line to explain the failure of markets to organise transactions between vertically related, technologically separable stages of production. Under certain conditions, markets are more efficient because they can mediate without paying the costs of managers, accountants or personnel departments. Under other conditions, a market mechanism becomes so cumbersome that it is less efficient than a bureaucracy.

In a perfectly competitive market, transactions are carried out without transaction costs. Information is freely available, decision-making is rational, there are always alternative suppliers and buyers, and there are no carry-over effects from one period to the other of a specific transaction between two parties in the market. When these conditions do not prevail, transaction costs emerge because there is a need to devote efforts to organising, carrying out and controlling transactions among independent actors. The transaction cost approach tries to explain the institutional forms, that is the 'governance structure' (market, hierarchy or intermediate forms) of these transactions. This perspective suggests that monopolies can result from transactional efficiency reasons. It therefore complements the neo-Austrian approach in challenging the long-held suspicion of monopoly and oligopoly in traditional welfare economics.

Further typologies: clans and networks

Coase (1937) made a sharp delineation of markets and hierarchies, but other typologies were later developed. Ouchi developed the 'clan'. Industrial organisations can, in some instances, rely to a great extent on socialisation as the principal mechanism of mediation or control, and this 'clan' form can be very efficient in mediating transactions between interdependent individuals. Ouchi argues that in certain organisations, e.g. Japanese firms, it is not necessary to measure performance to control or direct employees, since the employees' natural (socialised) inclination is to do what is best for the firm. It is also unnecessary to derive explicit, verifiable measures of value added, since rewards are distributed according to non-performance-related criteria which are relatively inexpensive to determine (e.g. length of service). Ouchi regards the critical elements of efficiency to be:

- ambiguity of individual performance measurement;
- congruence of employee's and employer's goals.

Market relations are efficient when there is little ambiguity over performance, so the parties can tolerate relatively high levels of opportunism or goal incongruence. Bureaucratic relations are efficient when both performance ambiguity and goal incongruence are moderately high. A clan achieves efficiency when there is high performance ambiguity and low opportunism. The requirements of each organisational form are outlined in Figure 2.3.

Reciprocity is defined as each party regarding the transaction as equitable. Prices are regarded as a highly sophisticated form of information for decision-making. It is acknowledged that 'correct' prices are difficult to arrive at, particularly when technological interdependence, novelty or other forms of ambiguity obscure the boundary between tasks and individuals. Rules are generally specific to individual problems and therefore a large number may be required, with exceptions being referred upwards. Under uncertainty or complexity, the number of exceptions is so great that the system becomes overloaded, with a consequent reduction in decision quality. On the other hand, traditions are implicit rules, stated only generally. Hence they are crude in terms of performance evaluation, but may provide a uniform philosophy, etc., and therefore provide 'a very elegant and complete form of control' (*Ouchi*, 1993).

Figure 2.3: An organisational framework

Mode of control	Normative requirements	Informational requirements
Market	Reciprocity	Prices
Bureaucracy	Reciprocity Legitimate authority	Rules
Clan	Reciprocity Legitimate authority Common values and beliefs	Traditions

Source: *Ouchi* (1993)

A network is a further common typology. A network is said to exist where the parties to the exchange are separate entities, but stable long-term relationships exist between the parties. Thompson (1993) rationalises clans and networks by classifying Ouchi's bureaucracy and clan as hierarchical–competitive and hierarchical–co-operative systems respectively, and classifying markets and networks as independent–competitive and independent–co-operative systems respectively (Figure 2.4).

Figure 2.4: Organisational form and approach to relationships

Organisational form	**Approach to relationships**	
	Competitive	*Co-operative*
Independent	Classic market	Network structure
Hierarchical	Bureaucracy	Clan

NHS governance structures

Lapsley (1993) argues that the NHS has been transformed from a 'clan' form of governance to a market model. The NHS has been characterised as an organisation which has been dominated by the medical profession (*Bourn and Ezzamel*, 1986; *Burke and Goddard*, 1990). Bourn and Ezzamel describe the medical profession as a clan; they argue that the NHS is typified by high goal congruence on the part of the medical profession and by high performance ambiguity (which is tolerated by clan members) and that this has given rise to the 'clan'. The medical profession was seen as one distinct, dominant sub-culture within a complex organisation (an 'enucleated bureaucracy'). This model of governance led to unnecessarily lengthy delays in decision-making, to behaviour which was geared to problem avoidance rather than solution and to 'institutionalised stagnation' (*Griffiths*, 1983).

These criticisms gave rise to the reform of the NHS hierarchy by implementation of the 'general management model which emphasised the importance of new accounting controls'. The medical clan under the 'management budgeting' initiative would have financial responsibilities within the formal hierarchy of the NHS.

This was largely a story of failure due to inadequate resources, an over-ambitious timescale and limited appreciation of the complexities and nuances of introducing such a substantive change in the face of strong professional independence (*Perrin,* 1988). Similarly, management budgeting's successor, 'resource management', made 'slow and patchy progress' (*Packwood,* 1991). It would appear that, as predicted by *Bourn and Ezzamel*, the control exerted by the medical clan (as constrained within the 'enucleated bureaucracy') retained an important role in the governance of the NHS throughout the attempt to implement an explicit, rules-based, managerial hierarchy in the 1980s.

The 1989 White Paper prescribed a market solution for the regulation of the NHS – the creation of an internal or quasi-market in health care (*DoH,* 1989a). *Lapsley* contrasts the changes in governance modes in the NHS with those of the private sector (Figure 2.5).

Figure 2.5: Dominant modes of governance – an inversion of private sector and NHS experiences

Private sector	*National Health Service*
Markets	Clan-based/culture control
↓	↓
Hierarchies	Hierarchies
↓	↓
Corporate cultures	Markets

Notes:

- It is important to note that these alternative modes of governance are described as dominant, i.e. markets, hierarchies proponents would recognise that hybrid forms of governance may exist and that there may be a mixture of modes of governance at any point in time.
- It is not suggested that these shifts occurred in parallel. The switch from markets to hierarchies in the private sector has been documented by, for example, *Chandler* (1977) as occurring to a large degree at the end of the last century and the early part of this century, whereas the NHS was not established until 1947. The important issue is the inversion *per se*, not the time frame.

Source: *Lapsley* (1993)

Lapsley points out that, while the aim of the internal market is to increase the efficiency of healthcare provision, and thereby to increase the overall level of patient care without concomitant additional resources, it has been criticised as being inappropriate on a number of grounds. In terms of the markets and hierarchies theory, the transaction costs of operating such a system are high. Usually the transactions involved in the process of market exchange are rather straightforward and the associated contract is easily specified by a verbal agreement. As the British Medical Association (BMA) has pointed out, this is not the case in healthcare.

> *'Contracts for specified services implies viable packaging arrangements which meet every eventuality. Flexibility would be essential to meet the great variation in general health status among different patients requiring the same package. A young fit adult with a hernia would require less overall hospital treatment than an elderly, unstable diabetic with the same condition.'* *BMA* (1989)

Where transactions are multi-dimensional, and outcomes are contingent upon an uncertain environment or 'state of nature', then the associated contracts (which *Williamson* refers to as 'contingent claims contracts') will be difficult to write, implement and enforce and the associated transaction costs will be high. This may well be the case in the NHS internal market. More specifically, high transaction costs are associated with the specification of contracts because:

- there is considerable uncertainty, not only over the cause and effect of certain treatments, but also because of the unpredictable nature of much non-elective health care;
- the sheer scale of the number of contracts which would be required to be placed on a cost per case contracting system places limits on decision-makers, both purchasers and providers;
- there is scope for opportunistic behaviour within this system (*Burke and Goddard*, 1990; *Bartlett*, 1991). Although in principle complete cost per case contracts could be specified, the associated transaction costs due to the increased costs of administration and information processing would probably add significantly to the average costs of running the health service. On the other hand, block contracts will not relate price to every eventuality. This incompleteness leaves scope for opportunistic behaviour which in turn will lead to costly medical audit and/or performance targets which will be expensive to administer.

The focus of this research study is the major difficulties for health-care providers in generating sufficiently precise costing information to enable appropriate contracts to be made.

Now that decisions on levels of activity lie within the hands of purchasers and providers, the position of the medical clan will be weakened, but this may prove to be inappropriate, in Ouchi's terms, on account of the perceived high goal congruence within the medical profession and the ambiguity over what constitutes good performance in healthcare. Furthermore, the implementation of a market mechanism with high transaction costs may fail and require some form of hierarchical or rules-based intervention to reduce or minimise such costs. It is also quite possible that, in the move from a bureaucratic or clan form of NHS organisation, networks using co-operative relationships may be paramount rather than the classic market. Pricing is crucial within markets, but rules, traditions or relationships may emerge as dominant in the new NHS.

2.6 Summary

Markets provide a mechanism for allocating resources. Perfectly competitive markets, according to neo-classical economics, provide the most efficient means of resource distribution. The neo-Austrian school, on the other hand, propounds the benefits arising from the competitive process *per se*. Advocates of contestable markets go a stage further and argue that, in terms of efficiency, contestable markets can compare favourably with the neo-classical perfect competition model.

Healthcare systems are subject to substantial state intervention. The reasons often given for such extensive intervention relate to market failure in relation to the neo-classical model and equity considerations. However, that is not to say that healthcare systems cannot benefit from the 'competitive process' nor achieve some of the efficiency gains of contestable markets. The internal market arrangements of the NHS, while not removing the financing of healthcare from general taxation, introduce competition between healthcare providers. Healthcare purchasers (DHAs and GPFHs) are expected to place contracts with providers who 'offer the best value'.

Consideration of transaction cost economics leads to investigation of alternative governance structures. Efficiency gains from competition must outweigh transaction costs if more or improved healthcare is to be gained through the NHS internal market. The NHS internal market will weaken the medical 'clan', although high transaction costs may require some form of hierarchical or rule-based intervention to reduce or minimise such costs. The internal market may exhibit features more akin to networks than the classical market.

Within markets, the price mechanism is crucial to the achievement of efficiency gains. Markets (whether taken from a neo-classical, neo-Austrian or contestable market perspective) operate via price signals. The scope for realising efficiency savings in the NHS internal market and the price mechanism necessary for driving the NHS towards such efficiencies are considered in the next chapter.

3

Economic Efficiency and Pricing Mechanisms

3.1 Introduction

The NHS internal market was introduced to promote efficiency. This chapter examines the scope for economic efficiency in the NHS. Price mechanisms, the basis of market operation, are then considered. Healthcare pricing theory and experience is examined in the light of the market's espoused efficiency aims and the prescribed cost-based pricing regime set out by the Department of Health.

3.2 Economic efficiency and the NHS

The aim of efficiency is firmly rooted in the NHS reforms. The concept of an internal market for healthcare in the UK had been propounded some years earlier by an American economist who saw its principal advantage as efficiency.

> *'The theory behind such a scheme is that managers would then be able to use resources most efficiently. They could buy services from producers who offered good value. They could use the possibility of buying outside as bargaining leverage to get better performance from their own providers. They could sell off assets such as valuable land in order to redeploy their capital most effectively. Unlike the normal bureaucratic model, they would not get money for doing a poor job with what they have.... The underbedded areas could buy services from the overbedded areas if, in their judgement, that was the way to get the best deal for their patients. The flow of services to people could be adjusted smoothly and rapidly without the need for facilities to be built or closed.'*
>
> *Enthoven* (1985)

Incentives for economic efficiency

Enthoven saw the structure of the pre-reform NHS as holding perverse incentives to efficiency: the efficiency trap; NHS waiting lists; new facilities; and GP referrals.

The efficiency trap

In the pre-reform NHS 'efficient' hospitals were in effect penalised for treating more patients – 'the efficiency trap'. If a hospital increased admissions by higher bed utilisation, the efficiency indicators of average cost per case and average cost per patient day would improve through the spreading of fixed costs over a larger workload. However, the overall fixed budget would be overspent because of the increase in variable costs.

> '*A District that develops an excellent service in some specialty that attracts more referrals is likely to get more work without getting more resources to do it. A District that does a poor job will 'export' patients and have less work, but not correspondingly less resources for its reward.... In a rational economic model, those whose quality of service attracts more patients would get paid [for doing the extra work] a negotiated amount that they agreed makes the effort worthwhile.*'
>
> *Enthoven* (1985)

In the internal market the efficiency trap is alleviated to some extent through funding health authorities according to their resident populations and then enabling money to flow with the patient. The extent to which the 'efficiency trap' remains will depend on the nature of the contracts placed and how they are priced.

NHS waiting lists

Enthoven argues that there is status in waiting lists which provides further perverse incentives to efficiency.

> '*A consultant's NHS waiting list creates a demand for his services by private pay patients. Thus clearing a waiting list is directly opposed to the economic interest of the consultant.*' *Enthoven* (1985)

He goes on to argue that the waiting list phenomenon is aggravated by the fact that GPs referring patients to other districts with low waiting lists risk antagonising consultants in their own districts: GPs who want a good reception for their patients when they need it must play the referral game to the satisfaction of consultants in their own districts.

In the internal market, the workload should be determined through the placing of contracts.

New facilities

In the pre-reformed NHS, hospital managers and consultants risked weakening their case for new facilities if they reduced the waiting list by referring patients to other hospitals with excess capacity. As Enthoven pointed out, the cure for this incentive is to structure the budgeting system so that resources are determined by an impersonal mechanism that does not provide more resources for less efficiency.

In the internal market, the viability of new capital developments depends on their future generation of contract income to cover costs (including a return on capital), and a business case must therefore be made.

GP referrals

GPs have weak or no incentives to reduce referrals. However, the introduction of GP fundholding in the internal market does provide an incentive to reduce referrals for fundholding services – the GP can use savings made on his GPFH budget for the benefit of his GP practice.

Enthoven concluded that it was in the area of incentives that the NHS structure was weakest.

> *'It relies on dedication and idealism.... But it offers few positive incentives to do a better job for the patients, and it has some perverse ones.'*
> *Enthoven* (1985)

In proposing an internal market system he accepted that it 'would not include powerful incentives for management to make efficiency-improving changes, but it would remove some of the disincentives'.

Scope for economic efficiency

There are two distinct uses of the term efficiency. On the supply side, there is the concept of productive or technical efficiency, which refers to the reductions in the cost per unit of a good or service. Technical efficiency in the provision of healthcare exists where the costs of producing or maintaining a given output are minimised and the utility of individuals' preferences is maximised for a given cost. On the demand side, there is the more general concept of allocative efficiency. This term encompasses productive efficiency but also measures the extent to which the output of service is consistent with consumer preferences *(Robinson,* 1988). Allocative efficiency considers how to maximise the benefit from available resources *(Mooney,* 1992). Thus allocative or 'high-level' efficiency addresses the question of whether the level and mix of services does most good with the resources available, i.e. meets consumer demands. In the context of the NHS internal market, the overall level of financial resources is determined outside the market, but it is still important to consider whether the best package of healthcare is delivered to consumers within the budget constraints. The optimal mix requires the maximisation of patient welfare. In order to achieve maximisation of patient welfare not only must the cost per unit of healthcare be minimised, but also the service mix, including access to services and their quality, must be consistent with consumer demands.

By allowing funds to flow to healthcare providers according to the contracted workload undertaken, the efficiency trap for an individual hospital can be removed, but extra funds gained by one provider will be at the expense of another. Thus in order for benefits to arise to the NHS as a whole, incentives must be given to encourage allocative and productive efficiency. There are three specific sources of potential productive efficiency gain that might be expected to follow from the introduction of the NHS internal market: reductions in X-inefficiency; lower costs from economies of scale and scope; and lower costs from reductions in input prices. In addition, the reforms may improve allocative efficiency through increased consumer choice with a more varied range of services more closely meeting consumer preferences.

Reductions in X-inefficiency

Most organisations display different degrees of X-inefficiency, that is, a divergence between actual and minimum costs.

> *'For a variety of reasons people and organisations normally work neither as hard nor as effectively as they could. In situations where competitive pressure is light, many people will trade the disutility of greater effort, of search, and the control of other peoples' activities for the utility of feeling less pressure and of better interpersonal relations. But in situations where competitive pressures are high and hence the costs of such trades are also high, they will exchange less of the disutility of effort for the utility of freedom from pressure, etc.'* *Liebenstein* (1966)

A firm's failure to adopt the most efficient means of production will lead to higher prices, a loss of custom and reduced profitability. In the NHS there is evidence that hospitals vary in the extent to which they achieve efficient levels of capacity utilisation. Failure to maximise the use of operating theatres, beds and staff time have been highlighted (*National Audit Office*, 1987; *Yates*, 1987). The Audit Commission has criticised poor use of day-case facilities (*Audit Commission*, 1990) and called for the rationalisation of the capacity of pathology laboratories (*Audit Commission*, 1991).

Lower costs from economies of scale and scope

Economies of scale arise when the cost per unit of output falls as the scale of production increases. There have been surprisingly few econometric studies of health service cost–output relationships in the UK. In 1989, *Wagstaff* concluded that those which had been carried out suggested a U-shaped cost function with minimum costs reached at 430 beds or more (*Wagstaff*, 1989). However, a more recent study in the UK indicates that there are decreasing returns to scale up to a capacity of 715 beds (*Bartlett and Le Grand*, 1992), but this study ignored capital costs. A recent US study has also found diseconomies of scale in hospitals with low capacity (*Vita*, 1990). Nevertheless, practical experience, for example provision of certain multi-district or regional specialties at a small number of designated sites, suggests that there are likely to be cost savings from rationalising services on fewer sites. In 1972, *Berki* expressed the following view when trying to make sense of hospital cost functions:

> *'Economies of scale exist, may exist, may not exist, or do not exist, but in any case, according to theory, they ought to exist.'* *Berki* (1972)

Twenty years later, it is still difficult to validate the theory.

More recently, economic analysis has developed the concepts of subadditivity and economies of scope.

> *'A cost function is subadditive for a particular output vector y when y can be produced more cheaply by a single firm than by any combination of smaller firms.'* *Baumol, Panzar and Willig* (1988)

However, subadditivity is very difficult to analyse – it cannot be recognised by looking at a mathematical expression or graph of the cost function, and indeed it requires knowledge of all possible cost functions for an output vector smaller than *y*.

Economies of scope also developed from the study of scale economics (*Panzar and Willig*, 1975). This concept refers to situations in which the cost of producing two products in combination C(A,B), is less than the total cost of producing each product separately, C(A,O) + C(O,B). *Panzar and Willig* (1977, 1979) showed that the ideas of economies of scope and overall and product-specific returns to scale are inextricably related. Economies of scope and overall and decreasing average incremental costs in each product line together imply both overall scale economies and strict subadditivity.

In the NHS internal market it is likely that considerable economies of scope are present. For example, if products are taken as specific hospital treatments it is obviously more efficient to provide a number of ENT procedures rather than just one or two (the consultant and his medical team can cover a wide range of treatments; indeed, such a range is necessary to maintain medical skills).

Reductions in input prices

Over and above any reductions in costs per unit resulting from increases in productivity (discussed under X-inefficiency above), it may be possible through competition to reduce the *prices* of inputs. According to economic theory, competition in the market for factor inputs ensures that that no factor earns a surplus rent payment as a result of monopoly or other barriers to competition. In the conditions existing before the reforms, input prices have been relatively invariant across hospitals, owing to the centralised and administrative system of input procurement and wage bargaining. The introduction of trust hospitals able to determine their own rates of pay and conditions will lead to input price variations for labour which account for over 75 per cent of the costs (excluding capital costs) of the average hospital. However, the freedom for individual hospitals to determine their own rates of pay has been identified as a potential source of cost escalation (*Barr et al.*, 1989; *Mayston*, 1990). Further efficiency savings may result from changes in the skill mix, for example, utilising more staff nurses and fewer sisters, etc.

Consumer choice, quality of services and equity

In competitive markets, the responsiveness to consumer demands is taken to be a necessary prerequisite for financial success and/or survival. In the NHS internal market, the purchasers of healthcare are DHAs and GPFHs, not the consumers of healthcare. GPFHs may have discussions with patients about appropriate forms of hospital treatment, and this, together with the greater freedom for patients to change GPs, offers enhanced consumer choice. However, most healthcare will be covered by contracts placed by district health authorities, and the link between consumer demands and contracts placed for service provision is weak. There is a danger that cost-conscious DHAs faced with cash-limited budgets and GPFHs will pursue least-cost service contracts. In an attempt to avoid this, measuring quality is embodied in the internal market arrangements (*DoH*, 1989a). DHAs have to ensure that service contracts include details of the facilities to be made available, criteria for the admission and discharge of patients, maximum waiting times and measures of the quality of clinical care (*DoH*, 1989e).

Equity considerations are important in healthcare and can influence efficiency. Equity can be viewed as having two principal dimensions over and above the provision of a minimum level of healthcare. Horizontal equity is concerned with the equal treatment of equals (i.e. providing the same amount of healthcare for individuals who are identical in terms of all relevant characteristics such as age, sex, health status, geographical location, etc.). The second dimension of equity concerns the 'unequal treatment of unequals' *(McAlistair*, 1994) or vertical equity. The pursuit of vertical equity may require a trade-off with efficiency. McAlistair gives health prevention as an example where it may be the case that reducing risks by a little for the majority of the population will save fewer lives than if the same level of resources was concentrated on the minority most at risk. In the internal market, differential access in clinical activities could arise between geographical areas if trade in clinical services results in some specialties becoming concentrated at a smaller number of hospitals. There is also the danger that the internal market could distort the pattern of service provision remaining in the geographical area. For example, easily specified services covering minor elective surgery – involving short stays and minimal complications after discharge – may appear more attractive to managers than some forms of longer-stay, less predictable, geriatric care. Service planning priorities may be distorted.

In 1989 there were undoubtedly inefficiencies within the NHS, not surprisingly in an organisation which had weak or perverse efficiency incentives and spent over £27bn per annum. The internal market arrangements offer a potential means of reducing some production inefficiencies, but there are also wider problems relating to access to services and the mix of health services if allocative efficiency is to be addressed.

3.3 Price mechanisms

Markets require a price mechanism. In the NHS internal market, an appropriate pricing mechanism is necessary to provide signals to (potential) competitors and to direct purchasers to efficient providers.

Incentives to respond to price signals

In competitive markets suppliers are motivated to achieve productive efficiency and to respond to market signals by the desire to maximise profit. In the NHS internal market, because of the absence of claimants to residual income, it could be argued that suppliers will face weak incentives to maximise profits which could lead to productive and allocative inefficiency. On the other hand, *Griffiths* (1983) argued that even the pre-reform NHS was not that different from the private sector:

> *'In many organisations in the private sector, profit does not immediately impinge on large numbers of managers below Board level. They are concerned with levels of service, quality of product, meeting budgets, cost improvement, productivity, motivating and rewarding staff, research and development, and the long-term viability of the undertaking. All things that Parliament is urging on the NHS.'*

Furthermore, in a competitive market the scope for discretionary behaviour is severely limited by the erosion of excess profit in the move towards equilibrium. Even in the absence of the profit-maximising objective, *Ferguson and Posnett* (1990) claim that the best guard against organisational slack is the operation of the competitive process itself. Indeed, proponents of contestable market theory argue that the maximisation of competition for public service markets and the threat of possible new entrants is the single most effective means of ensuring maximum efficiency in service provision, preventing excess profits being earned by the exploitation of captive consumers, and ensuring adequate quality of service *(Bailey,* 1981; *Baumol, Panzar and Willig,* 1988; *Bailey and Baumol,* 1984).

Non-price competition

If the NHS internal market approach is to achieve its espoused efficiency aims, it is essential that competition is on the basis of price and not on the basis of non-price factors. Marketing, advertising, product differentiation, and market segmentation, all forms of non-price competition, dominated US hospital competition in the 1980s (*Higgins*, 1991). Non-price competition for physicians and patients is inflationary because it contributes to redundant and under-utilized services and technology (*Luft*, 1986; *Robinson,* 1987). Instead of seeing overbuilt hospitals in competitive urban markets in the US going out of business, hospital closures in the 1980s tended to be either rural hospitals or urban hospitals serving a disproportionate share of indigent patients (*Hollingsworth and Hollingsworth*, 1987). *Robinson and Luft* (1985) conclude that evidence from the US proves that non-price competition in healthcare leads not to reduced cost and enhanced efficiency, but to excess capacity, duplication of services, increased levels of amenity and higher costs. Higgins sums up the problem:

> *'In most hospital markets today, competing to attract well-insured patients yields greater financial rewards than efforts to improve efficiency.'*
> *Higgins* (1991)

Price controls and regulation

In perfectly competitive markets the manager has no power over price, being compelled to accept the prevailing one, since price is determined by the interaction of all buyers and sellers. However, the NHS internal market is inevitably, after many years of central planning, characterised by local monopolies.

> *'Although there is probably a high degree of competition for services such as elective surgery, where many patients are prepared to travel, and for*

other services in densely populated urban areas, there will be considerable monopoly or oligopoly power in some services outside conurbations and for regional and supra-regional services.'

Department of Health (1989f)

In a monopoly situation there is an incentive for the monopolist to raise prices above the competitive level and thus earn monopoly (super-normal) profits. Oligopolistic suppliers often enjoy a protected position afforded by barriers to the entry of new suppliers and consequently may also be able to enjoy super-normal profits. In acute healthcare provision, high capital investment, asset specificity and technical skills can provide entry barriers, particularly for the more complex treatments. In an oligopoly, pricing is a question of strategy, and the outcome of any particular form of pricing depends on the reaction of rivals. As shown in Figure 3.1, very few acute healthcare services are likely to have any resemblance to the perfect competition model of many buyers and sellers. The market for GPFH procedures (particularly in the large conurbations) would be the closest: in this market, providers would largely be price takers, and competitive pressure could force healthcare providers to keep their prices low.

Figure 3.1: Degree of concentration, market structure and characteristics

	SEVERAL PROVIDERS	*A FEW PROVIDERS*	*ONE PROVIDER*
Product (healthcare services)	Simple elective treatment, i.e. reasonably homogeneous product (GPFH procedures)	More advanced elective treatment. Emergency treatment in conurbations	Supra-regional/ regional specialties. Emergency and more advanced elective treatments outside conurbations
Different'ion	Some differentiation by place, GP preference, etc.	Differentiation of products	Differentiation of products
Purchasers	Many GPFHs and several DHAs	One or a few DHAs	One or a few DHAs

Price taker ◄────► Price maker

Low entry barriers ◄────► Entry barriers

On the other hand, the market for some highly specialised services would be monopolistic and healthcare providers could keep prices artificially high. Without regulation, the DoH believed the market would be subject to abuse by monopoly suppliers at least in the short run. Even in the long run, financial and other barriers to entry deter new hospitals from setting up in competition with established ones, and therefore contestable markets may be difficult to ensure.

Consequently, pricing methods (controls) must be designed which prevent the abuse of monopoly power if the internal market is to encourage economic efficiency. Two possible pricing approaches are a central price schedule and a set of pricing rules based on individual provider cost.

A central price schedule

A central price schedule could be imposed by central government. Contracts would then be negotiated for the volume of cases to be treated in a given period and for the quality or amenity characteristics of care. In the United States, fixed-rate reimbursement has been a feature of the Medicare system since 1983. Although a fixed-rate payment schedule may be successful in reducing the level of hospital costs, it cannot be used to enhance competition or to reduce the importance of non-price competition. These issues are considered below in a competitive environment and in a monopolistic environment.

Under a central price schedule a competitive provider will have an incentive to minimise the costs of production, but

> *'There is no unique "minimum cost" for providing healthcare services when the intensity and quality of care can vary. Defining any particular reimbursement rate simultaneously defines the quality, intensity or amenity level of the care provided.'* *Joskow* (1983)

In the unlikely event that the schedule reimbursement rate is greater than the average cost of treatment, competition for patients will drive up expenditures on amenities and hospital resource use until any surplus of payment over costs is eroded (all excess profits are transferred to consumers). On the other hand, if the schedule reimbursement rate is less than current costs, as would be appropriate if cost reduction is the aim, then all competing hospitals within a local market will reduce expenditures per case up to the point at which costs are exactly equal to the schedule rate (the level of amenity and resource use are reduced).

A profit-maximising monopoly provider under a schedule reimbursement rate will continue to minimise costs, and will continue to provide the minimum level of amenity consistent with demand. Any surplus of reimbursement over costs will be converted to profit. If the provider is non-profit-making, on-the-job rents will apply.

Schedule rates would therefore generate cost savings only for those hospitals where the fixed rate is less than current costs. One possible response would be for hospitals to change the classification of patients into more lucrative treatment categories, a practice known as 'DRG creep' in the USA where it is prevalent (*Carter and Ginsberg*, 1985). A central price schedule would also be difficult to achieve because of regional and historical cost variations; these can be considerable (*CIPFA*, 1990). More fundamentally, a central price schedule could not be used to encourage economic efficiency in the NHS internal market as prices would not guide purchasers (DHAs and GPFHs) to their most productive use and reward cost-effective services. As outlined above, one of the ways in which monopoly rents are captured by monopolists, especially non-profit-making ones, is via cost increases. If these become embodied in schedule rates, then 'average' X-inefficiency is not penalised, thus nullifying one of the main potential benefits of enhanced competition.

Individual provider cost

An alternative approach is to base contract prices on individual provider cost. Provider cost can be either retrospective or prospective. Under a system of retrospective reimbursement at full cost, a hospital subsequently receives payment in full from purchasers for all reasonable expenditure incurred. Experience in the USA has shown that retrospective reimbursement encourages long lengths of hospital stay, excessive diagnostic testing, etc. (*Rosko and Broyles*, 1987; *Guterman and Dobson*, 1986; *Sloan et al.*, 1983; *Newhouse and Byrne*, 1988).

A system of payment based on retrospective reimbursement promotes inefficiency and cost escalation. It would also be extremely difficult for purchasers to keep within cash-limited allocations. A system which bases prices on prospective provider cost, on the other hand, would provide greater control while still enabling purchasers to be guided by price.

It is therefore understandable that the NHS Management Executive decided to instruct NHS providers to set prices equal to prospective cost plus a rate of return on capital (*NHSME*, 1990). Indeed, such pricing is in line with the economist's approach to public sector pricing.

3.4 The economist's approach to public sector pricing

Cost-based pricing

If a private sector firm pursues profit maximisation, this has clear implications for the prices it will charge. They will be profit maximising prices, not necessarily in the neo-classical matching of marginal cost (MC) to marginal return (MR), but in the sense that the firm feels its way by a process of trial and error towards prices that maximise the firm's profit (the competitive process). For a public sector organisation, particularly a monopolistic one, the pursuit of maximum profit is not necessarily an appropriate objective.

After the Second World War, economists argued that nationalised industries should use marginal cost pricing. However, it became clear that nationalised industries operated in an environment where most firms' prices were not equal to MC. If nationalised industries set prices equal to MC when prices were higher in the private sector, this would lead to a misallocation of society's resources. Recognising this, economists developed the general theory of 'the second best'. In a second-best world, where in the private sector price exceeds MC, nationalised industries should emulate the behaviour of private sector firms. Thus if in the private sector prices exceed MC by 6 per cent then public sector organisations should set their prices on the same basis. In this way a Pareto optimal allocation of resources is still assured even in the second-best world.

In theory, MC to the economist is the derivative of the total cost function or the increase in total costs which results from the production of one extra unit of output. However, in the real world there are indivisibilities. For example, for a hospital with empty beds in a ward, the extra cost of another patient is very low. When the beds are full, on the other hand, the MC of another patient is the cost of opening up a new ward. To adhere strictly to MC pricing would result in most purchasers paying very low amounts and one extremely unfortunate purchaser paying a very high price. In addition, in calculating MC some account must be taken of capital costs. The hospital must be able to replace its capital equipment and building stock. A related point is that hospitals are likely to be subject to scale economies, i.e. the long-run average cost (LRAC) curve is downward sloping. Consequently, if average costs are declining, MC must be less than average cost. If the hospital sets a price equal to MC and charges a price of P_1 (see Figure 3.2), losses will result. For the organisation to break even, prices must be set at P_2. The definition of cost includes a normal return on capital and, therefore, breakeven using LRAC really means that the hospital is making zero super-normal profits.

Figure 3.2: Marginal or average cost pricing

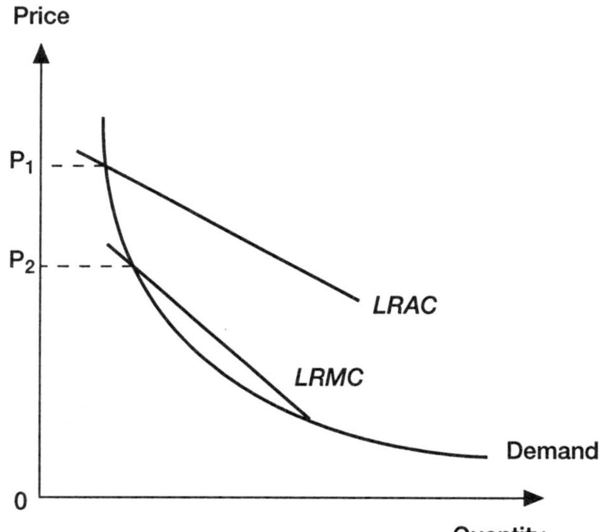

In line with this reasoning, pricing in the NHS internal market is set to achieve financial targets imposed on hospitals. The financial target is explicit for NHS trusts (a 6 per cent return on the current cost of assets). In directly managed units (DMUs) it is embodied in the pricing rules which require cost-based prices to include capital charges (current cost depreciation plus 6 per cent interest). The NHSME is seeking to imitate the pricing of efficient competition and prevent the abuse of monopoly power.

Openness in costing and pricing

In theory at least, purchasers will be guided by price to the most 'efficient' provider and providers will be encouraged to improve efficiency (as long as markets are contestable: *Baumol et al.*, 1988). However, in order to reduce the likelihood that in monopoly situations cost-plus pricing will encourage cost-enhancing inefficiency, openness in costing and pricing is required. *Culyer and Posnett* (1990) see such openness as a method of providing yardsticks to enable purchasers to assess contracts more fully. Yardstick competition is a device used by regulators which enables them to encourage efficiency in monopoly industries (*Kay and Vickers*, 1990). In the 1980s, NHS performance indicators were developed for a similar purpose. *Robinson* (1994) argues that with a system of yardstick competition in place, improvements in standards should be achievable through negotiation and mutually agreed action between purchasers and providers.

3.5 Summary

The internal market arrangements provide scope for reducing productive efficiency. However, the existence of monopolies, and difficulties in ensuring contestability, have led the NHS Management Executive to require prices to be determined on a full-cost basis with a return on capital. Developing cost methods for prices which reflect comparative efficiency is important if contracts are to encourage improvements in efficiency and drive the market towards a long-run equilibrium characterised by productive and allocative efficiency.

4

Accounting Choices and NHS Cost-based Pricing

4.1 Introduction

This chapter examines the accounting choices in compiling cost-based prices in the NHS. Accounting information for pricing decisions and appropriate cost 'products' are discussed before examining different methods of attributing hospital costs.

4.2 Absorption or marginal cost pricing

Absorption (full) cost pricing

There is general agreement that long-run pricing decisions should be based on the recovery of full cost if the organisation is to remain financially viable. Full (absorption) costs are based on normal volume and a normal mix of facilities. The full cost of a product (e.g. a specific service, test, procedure, visit, examination, case, discharge, etc.) includes the variable costs plus a 'fair' share of all fixed costs. In this respect all fixed-cost models involve some subjectivity in cost attribution and averaging techniques in multi-product organisations – 'fairness' is subject to interpretation and negotiation.

In the USA, *Govindarajan and Anthony* (1983) reported that 33 per cent of 501 firms surveyed used a cost-plus approach based on total cost. In the UK, *Drury et al.* undertook a survey which shows that 'cost' is defined in several different ways when computing cost-plus selling prices, and that total manufacturing cost is prevalent (*Drury* 1992).

A variant of full-cost (or absorption) pricing is rate of return pricing. Rate of return pricing, as prescribed for the NHS internal market, builds on cost that is 'normalised' for fluctuations in the rate of output and develops a profit mark-up that is related to a planned rate of return on capital employed.

Sizer (1989) rationalises the use of full costs in pricing decisions:

> *'Once commitments which entail continuing fixed costs have been entered into, management wants unit costs for pricing decisions which include a provision for recovery of total outlay according to some plan, e.g. use of absorption costing with fixed costs included in product cost on the basis of normal capacity.'*

It could also be argued that full-cost estimates for pricing purposes are quick and cheap to operate and that such an approach enables pricing to be delegated through simple costing rules *(Sizer,* 1989). The principles set out by the NHS Management Executive therefore accord with private sector practice: pricing for healthcare contracts should be based on costs; costs should generally be arrived at on a full-cost basis (including a 6 per cent real rate of return on capital); and there should be no planned cross-subsidisation between contracts (*NHSME*, 1990).

However, full-cost pricing and rate of return pricing give no guarantee of cost recovery or required profit, except when demand and competitive conditions are as anticipated when the costs (and mark-up) were established. Specific criticisms of full-cost pricing are:

- it tends not to take account directly of demand and assumes prices are simply a function of costs. A hospital must be sure it can achieve contracts at the volume of activity built into the full-cost prices;
- it fails to reflect competition adequately – the volume of sales achieved will depend on competition, not merely the hospital's own costs;
- it overplays the precision of attributed fixed costs and capital employed in a multi-product business. There is no uniquely appropriate way of allocating fixed costs and capital charges (current cost depreciation and interest) over the numerous services provided in a hospital;
- the attribution of common fixed costs provides only a very crude measure of the opportunity costs of using those resources;
- full-cost pricing is a long-run concept, but healthcare provision is subject to rapid technological and other changes in treatment patterns, and the incidence of illness can also fluctuate markedly;

- if prices are based on full cost, there is a danger that variations in non-price variables (e.g. waiting lists) are incorrectly evaluated.

Marginal pricing

On the other hand, the marginal cost approach to pricing decisions recognises that decision-making is essentially a process of choosing between competing alternatives, each with its own combination of income and costs; and that the relevant concepts to employ are future incremental costs and revenues and opportunity costs, not full costs which include past (sunk) costs. With marginal pricing the organisation seeks to fix its prices so as to maximise its total contribution to fixed costs and profit. The NHSME has stated that marginal cost contracts will represent only a small part of a provider's activity arising in the year from unplanned spare capacity.

> *'As prices should be based on full costs and costs should be allocated using assumed service levels, costing services at marginal cost rates will apply only for the pricing of marginal capacity in the short term. Hence such contracts would be tenable only for periods of less than one year. As a general rule one year's marginal capacity would be incorporated into the following year's assumed service level unless there are grounds for believing it would not be taken up by purchasers.'* *NHSME* (1990)

Marginal pricing holds a number of advantages:

- marginal costs more accurately reflect the future – if a hospital takes on (or loses) additional workload, its costs will increase (or decrease) by the marginal costs;
- when demand is highly elastic some of the prices determined by marginal costing would be considered uneconomic (if considered in relation to 'total' cost), but it may well be beneficial to the hospital to price services using a marginal approach;
- marginal costing may be more indicative of potential competitor cost (important in competitive or contestable markets);
- marginal pricing also enables a more aggressive pricing policy.

However, fixed costs are important, at least in the longer term. Total contribution from all products must cover fixed costs. On the other hand, it is not essential that each separate product or market should produce a contribution which is sufficient to cover attributed fixed costs and provide a normal profit, although this is, in effect, what the NHSME's pricing principles require.

The NHSME's principles were introduced to encourage efficiency and prevent the abuse of monopoly power. They are largely in line with what tends to happen in practice as a 'starting point' for pricing decisions in the private sector. *Baxter and Oxenfeldt*'s reasoning of the widespread use of cost-based pricing in 1968 seems equally applicable to the reformed NHS:

> *'The main attraction of cost plus is, of course, that it offers a means by which plausible prices can be found with ease and speed, no matter how many products the firm handles. Moreover, its imposing computations look factual and precise, and its prices may well seem more defensible on moral grounds than prices established by other means.'*

The principles are very broad: hospitals have considerable freedom to choose the product level at which costs should be attributed and to determine appropriate means of cost allocation and apportionment.

4.3 The product level

An essential feature of any market is a clear and unambiguous definition of the product to be traded. Hospital patients exhibit a vast variety of characteristics and therefore it could be argued that each patient is unique. However, it would not be possible to contract at an individual patient level on a prospective basis as DHAs have to manage a fixed cash limit allocation for the residents of their locality. Unlike insurance companies, DHAs would not be able to raise additional income by increasing premiums and, furthermore, the administrative costs of such systems would be high.

An important determinant of overall hospital costs (in addition to the volume of services) is the range of services to be offered. The NHS Management Executive recommended specialty-based block contracts for the majority of providers in 1991/92. This is largely because of difficulties in obtaining more detailed pricing and monitoring. However, 113 procedures, investigations and out-patient visits were prescribed for pricing GPFH contracts. In the longer term, if the internal market is to achieve efficiencies through the contracting environment, contracts will have to be related to patient volume and the range of treatments within specialties (the case mix).

Thus a classification of case mix which condenses the infinite variety of hospital patients into appropriate groups is required. For the operation of sound cost accounting systems, the set of products which constitutes the business of each hospital would form the basis of a cost control system and flexible budgeting. Each product would be identified in terms of a treatment plan and set services to be delivered to the patient. For example, a patient over seventeen years old hospitalised for a tonsillectomy might be expected to consume six meals, two days of hotel services, six hours of nursing care, twenty minutes of surgery, etc. Each element would be costed so as to produce in each patient treatment department an explosion of the hospital's forecast mix of cases in terms of each case type (product) and their cost. As actual patient load became known, variance analysis would reveal the extent to which costs incurred in each cost centre were above or below expected values. The variances would be due to:

- input prices (personnel, materials);
- volume (number of patients treated);
- case mix (types of patients treated);
- efficiency (usage of input factors);
- treatment pattern (variations in physician prescription of services).

From the point of view of cost accounting, the crucial test of an appropriate product definition is the ability to define the likely resource consumption of the patient.

Specialties

Individual clinical specialties cover a wide range of hospital treatments, from those undertaken as a day case with little resource input to those requiring many weeks of hospital stay and high usage of resources. Specialty cases, while initially having the practical advantage of being relatively easy to cost and therefore price, would not enable resource consumption to be clearly defined and would be an unsatisfactory level at which to contract. Contracting on a specialty in-patient day rather than an average specialty case would build in a crude adjustment for case mix within specialty, the more complex cases generally requiring longer lengths of stay. However, the difficulty of ensuring that lengths of stay are justified would require strong utilisation review and patient management.

Patient diagnosis groupings

Patient classifications based on diagnosis can be expected to synthesise the patient's symptoms and determine expected treatment. Standardised classifications of diagnoses have been available for many years through the World Health Organisation ICD schemes. Thus the obvious contender at the commencement of the internal market for future products was that of diagnosis-related groups (DRGs) developed in the USA at the Yale School of Management. Four major criteria were specified in DRG development:

- the groups should be comprehensive and mutually exclusive;
- it should be possible to allocate cases to groups on the basis of routinely collected information;
- the resulting groups should be clinically coherent;
- the groups should be homogeneous in their use of resources.

It was also considered desirable that there should be no more than 500 DRGs to comprehend the entire range of hospital in-patient work. In Britain, the evaluation of DRGs commenced in 1982 (*Sanderson et al.*,1989). The patients are classified according to one or more of the following variables: principal diagnoses, age, sex and discharge position. Difficulties arise in the use of different diagnostic and operative procedure coding systems in Britain and the USA and also the sometimes poor quality of data recording (a problem which the resource management projects have been addressing). The clinical acceptability of DRGs varies widely, both in relation to the DRGs themselves and the clinical specialties. For DRGs which comprise a single diagnosis or procedure there is general clinical understanding and acceptance; in some instances, however, it is difficult for the practising clinician to perceive any rationale to the grouping other than the need to aggregate miscellanea. The criticisms of the application of DRGs in the USA have led to proposed alternatives to, or improvements on, the DRG classifications. For example, severity of illness is not accommodated within DRGs, but it is felt that inner-city and teaching hospitals tend to admit cases which are more severe than average and therefore require correspondingly more resources to treat effectively. Possible variations to overcome subjectivity in the definition of measurement of severity and the costs of collecting the relevant information are discussed by *Bardsley et al.* (1989). In 1990, work had commenced on redefining DRGs for British clinical practice.

Patient treatment groups

Patient grouping for contracts could alternatively be based on patient treatment patterns rather than diagnosis. Such groupings would be particularly strong from the point of view of internal management control, but would have the disadvantage of not being readily available from existing patient coding and requiring considerable development work. Some hospitals in the USA operate such treatment plans and the RM sites in the late 1980s had been developing treatment protocols. Patient treatment plans would fit the cost accounting 'industrial' model most closely. Variances could be measured according to the differences from planned treatment. However, although treatment profiles have considerable merit from the point of view of cost accounting, the numerous plans would be difficult to form into viable packaging arrangements (product lines).

Product definition and the quality of services

Product definition and quality of services are interlinked. Products can be differentiated on grounds of service quality, and the level of product definition also has repercussions in terms of the need for patient management and utilisation review. Indicators of service quality are difficult to establish in the NHS. The internal market approach requires purchasers' specifications to include quality requirements (*DoH*, 1990e). Ideally, DHAs as the purchasers of healthcare should be concerned with health outcomes (final outputs). The input/output taxonomy for cancer chemotherapy is illustrated in Figure 4.1.

Figure 4.1: Input/output/throughput taxonomy

Chemotherapy for Cancer	
Inputs	Beds, staff, drugs, laboratory services, etc.
Intermediate outputs	Patients treated, number of chemotherapy sessions, survival post-treatment, malignancy removed
Final outputs	Normal lifestyle, re-admissions, quality of life, death

Source: Adapted from *Roberts* (1990)

In 1990, outcome and performance measures concentrated on intermediate outputs, e.g. number of patients treated. Hospitals often had generic quality standards which covered adherence to statutory standards; medical audit; human resources; other general standards including patient and purchaser satisfaction surveys and service-specific quality standards – but often final output measures were not available or were restricted to re-admissions.

4.4 Cost determination

Having established the appropriate approach to pricing and the products (cost units), there are a number of ways in which the total costs of the products can be determined. Basic prerequisites for cost determination are:

- an up-to-date analysis of the hospital, separating clinical specialties (or other contract categories) and support departments;
- accurate information systems providing:
  - financial and cost data for each specialty (contract categories) and support department;
  - statistical data for each specialty (contract categories) and support department;
- an appropriate cost attribution technique.

A simplified model of how services flow between departments within a hospital is shown (Figure 4.2). There are, in reality, numerous support departments and clinical specialties (a specialty may encompass wards, clinical teams, theatre, etc.). Each of these flows of service could be used as a basis of cost attribution. Each cost attribution method starts with the process of determining costs which are to be attributed. For example, in the USA, Medicare and Medicaid specify that certain costs are peripheral to the provision of health services to Medicare and Medicaid beneficiaries and therefore are not authorised for inclusion in attributed costs. Similarly, the NHSME excludes some costs from the contract costing and pricing process, e.g. some education and training costs.

Figure 4.2: A simple conceptual model for healthcare services

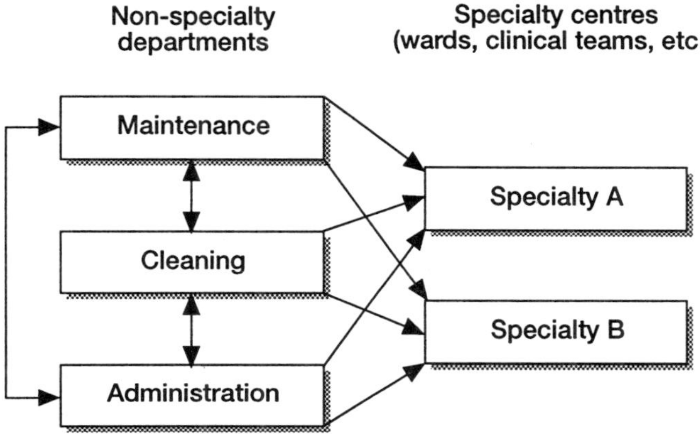

Traditional methods

There are four methods for cost attribution: direct apportionment; step-down, double or continuous distribution, and algebraic or reciprocal.

Direct apportionment

This method attributes costs directly to specialties (contract categories); it ignores the fact that most support departments also provide services to other support departments. It is therefore the least accurate form of cost determination. The Health Care Financing Administration in the USA does not permit the use of direct apportionment for cost reporting purposes (*Suver et al.*, 1992), but it does permit the other three. The NHSME did not prohibit the direct attribution of all costs to specialties for contract pricing when the costing principles were established in 1990.

Step-down method

This approach takes its name from the stair-step appearance of the calculation as the costs are attributed to production (clinical specialty) departments. This approach does recognise that support services provide services to other support departments.

The order in which departments are dealt with is subjective. After apportionment, the support department is considered closed; the method does not recognise all interrelationships between support departments. In the USA, the Medicare cost reporting forms contain a recommended step-down order and allocation bases (*Wise*, 1992). The majority of the NHS cost demonstration sites in 1990, outlined in Chapter 5, used the direct method described above.

Double or continuous distribution method

The above methods fail to account fully for interdepartmental services. Using double or multiple distribution, each support centre remains 'open' and costs can be reapportioned to support centres. The method may use two iterations (double) or the iterations may continue successively (continuous) until further apportionments result in immaterial changes.

The final apportionment to specialties is made successively. Each hospital's interpretation is likely to be unique: which departments to exclude; how many iterations; which apportionment bases to be used. This approach more precisely represents the interaction among the various departments, i.e. the patterns of actual activities and services, but it is not clear when to stop reapportioning to support departments or which order of priority to adopt.

The algebraic or reciprocal method

This method uses simultaneous equations to attribute costs most completely. The equations are mathematical representations of the known interrelationships between all departments. The results are more objective than those obtained using the other methods and require no assumptions regarding starting or stopping points. *Suver et al.* (1992) argue that it is the most defensible method for regulatory and negotiation purposes.

The resultant cost attribution from the differing methods may be minimal, and therefore management decisions such as the use of space may create wider variations than different accounting methods. However, *Howard* (1979) compared the reciprocal method with the step-down method for a six-month period on a test hospital; the differences in departmental costs varied by as much as 30 per cent.

In the NHS internal market, the direct specialty costs (consisting largely of direct ward costs and clinical teams) are likely to account for less than half of total costs, and therefore different cost attribution methods could provide significant differences. Furthermore, even if hospitals adopt the same method, differing apportionment bases, different starting points, etc., may be adopted. As the contract category (product level) becomes more closely defined, e.g. moves below specialty to procedure), the level of indirect costs will increase and increasingly complex systems of cost attribution will be required.

4.5 Development of the costing model

The hospital cost model could move closer to the industrial model whereby the cost of patient treatment departments (production areas) are distinguished from other departments, and the costs of patient groups are determined according to their costs accumulated in the various patient treatment departments. The cost of patient treatment departments would include the costs of the indirect service (overhead) departments. These costs would be attributed to patient treatment departments (wards, theatres, out-patient clinics, X-ray, etc.) using one of the four methods outlined earlier. The costs of intermediate products, e.g. ward cost per day, theatre cost per hour, etc., would then be used to compile 'final product' costs. This is similar to the developments at the original resource management sites and some US hospital accounting systems, which are considered in Chapter 5.

Activity-based costing

Activity-based costing (ABC) would require a more sophisticated approach than the traditional approaches to overhead attribution. ABC is a costing method originally developed in a manufacturing context to generate product costs. Its advocates argue that:

> *'the principles and methods ... are applicable to any significant collection of corporate resources in the manufacturing or service sector.'*
> *Cooper and Kaplan* (1988)

ABC involves the identification of the constituent activities (as opposed to departments) which consume organisational resources. These activities are individually costed and an appropriate measure (known as a cost driver) of the activity's workload is selected to permit the computation of activity cost rates (i.e. total activity cost/total cost driver volume). ABC is based on the premise that activities consume resources and products consume activities. An activity-based costing study in the NHS concluded that:

> *'In most departments a single driver or workload measure is not enough if true cost behaviour is to be modelled. Some activities in what are currently known as overhead areas are not related directly to a patient nor can they be deemed to be service costs and so should not be allocated to patient procedures through complex allocation routines via direct care departments. It is felt that ABC will generate more accurate costs for pricing than the traditional approaches.'* *HFMA* (1992)

Target costing

Target costing is widely used by Japanese companies. It is an approach driven by external market factors. A selling price is determined by marketing management prior to designing and introducing a new product. This price is set at a level that will permit the organisation to achieve a desired market share and sales volume. A desired profit margin is then deducted to determine the target maximum allowable product cost. In an industrial setting, product costs are computed based on design specifications and compared with target cost. If the projected product cost is above the target cost, then product designers focus on modifying the design of the product so that it becomes cheaper to produce.

This costing technique fits well with the Government's efficiency aims for the NHS internal market. If a hospital's existing treatments are more costly than those of alternative hospitals, it can examine treatment practices (e.g. length of stay, use of day-case facilities, etc.) and thereby reduce X-inefficiency. Similarly, in contestable markets, new entrants will compare their estimated treatment costs with those of existing providers.

Initially, owing to the lack of costing systems for elements of healthcare (nursing time, theatre usage, drugs, laboratory tests, etc.) and resource profiles for products (treatments), it was envisaged that most hospitals would determine costs at specialty level: little standard costing would be used and large elements of cost would be attributed through direct apportionment. In the longer term, a system which builds up the cost elements of healthcare and subsequently the cost of product lines could be developed. This approach would therefore be comparable with the industrial model for establishing product costs. The specialty cost approach with direct apportionment of overhead departments and multi-specialty treatment departments (pathology laboratories, X-ray, theatres, etc.) could be implemented relatively quickly and cheaply and enables product costs to be easily reconciled with the total cost of the hospital. On the other hand, it provides an imprecise measure of resource use which is likely to lack credibility and acceptability to clinicians and other healthcare professions. The extent of the imprecision depends on the methods adopted for absorbing overheads and attributing direct service department costs to contracts. More sophisticated approaches would provide the most precise measure of cost and be more likely to gain acceptance with clinicians. It would also assist medical audit, the quality review process and the introduction of flexible budgeting. However, the greater the emphasis on the industrial model (and particularly ABC within the industrial model), the more expensive and labour-intensive it is likely to be to introduce.

4.6 Summary

Accounting choices in NHS healthcare cost-based pricing relate to assessing cost relevance (e.g. full cost or marginal cost), the product level for cost and pricing purposes, and the approaches to be adopted in determining cost. In order for the internal market to achieve its efficiency aims, cost-based prices must both provide reasonable measures of resource consumption and facilitate meaningful comparisons between alternative providers. The product needs to be clearly defined (clinical specialties cover a number of disparate treatments) and both accurate and consistent methods of cost attribution used.

5
A Review of Healthcare Cost Information in 1990

5.1 Introduction

This chapter provides a review of healthcare cost information prior to the inception of the NHS internal market. As such, it provides an initial indication of the problems and the potential for cost accounting methods in pricing healthcare. After first considering the nature of healthcare cost behaviour, cost information available throughout the NHS and under specific initiatives is set out, including an outline of the 1990 UK cost demonstration sites. Finally, cost accounting in the USA, where a market approach to healthcare has been adopted, is examined and implications for contracting in the NHS internal market considered.

5.2 Cost behaviour

Hospital cost behaviour is difficult to identify. Each patient stay is unique and hospital costs relate not just to patients but also to empty beds. Figure 5.1 shows a hypothetical cost profile for an individual case and the turnover interval (the period between one patient being discharged and another one being admitted). Thus both the length of patient stay and the turnover interval are important in determining hospital costs, as well as the number and type of patients.

Direct treatment costs will normally be the highest at the beginning of the hospital stay and will fall as time passes. The residential costs will generally be constant over the whole period of stay of the patient. The costs of providing facilities will continue at a uniform rate throughout both the period of stay and the turnover interval while the bed remains empty. Parameters T, R, and F are likely to vary between different groups of patients, and if economies or diseconomies of scale are present R and F will vary according to the size of the relevant patient care unit within the hospital.

Establishing meaningful patient groups is extremely difficult. The actual shape of the cost-profile curve varies between specialties, and in particular at the sub-specialty or procedure level. Varying combinations of patients within specialties (the case mix) can have a major impact on direct costs. Identification of appropriate cost units (i.e. patient spells which are homogeneous as regards resource inputs and costs) provides a further area of difficulty, as discussed earlier in section 4.3. In 1990 there were few hospitals in the UK where the behaviour of costs in relation to activity had been researched and documented, and even fewer that used such information in a financial management system.

Figure 5.1: Cost incurred over effective length of patient stay

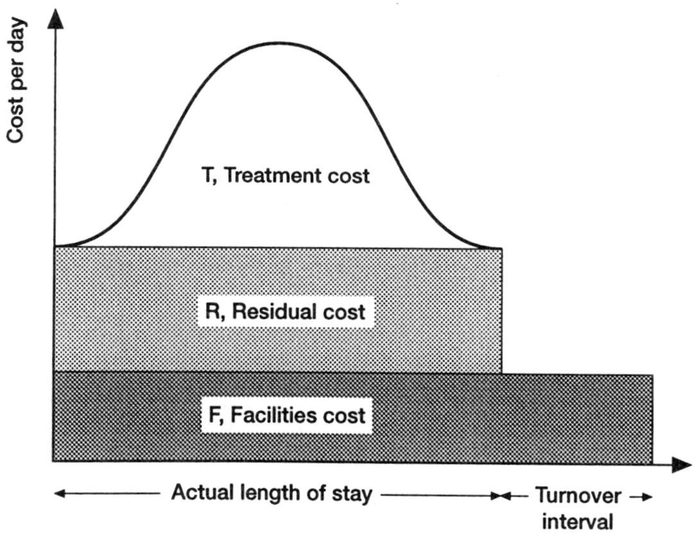

5.3 NHS cost information before the internal market

The NHS has had budgetary and cost systems since its earliest days, but they were designed primarily to ensure probity, control total expenditure and provide data to the Department of Health, rather than to facilitate pricing or to assess product cost recovery.

Cost analysis and reporting

Subjective analysis of costs

In the early decades of the NHS, cost analysis was limited to an analysis of actual costs by subjective expenditure categories (medical staff costs, nursing staff costs, drugs, travel expenses, etc.).

Functional costs and budgets

In 1974, in line with the change in organisational structures, the analysis of costs shifted to a functional basis (i.e. specialised professional services such as nursing services, pharmacy services, etc.), and functional budgets were introduced to help monitor compliance with budget limits by heads of functions. The 1982 NHS reorganisation created health units below district level and was soon followed by the Griffiths Inquiry (*Griffiths*, 1983). This recommended the appointment of general managers down to unit level, and consequently the cost and budget systems were decentralised to unit level. In the years preceding the internal market, the development of more sophisticated costing and budgeting had been supplementary to this functional control at unit level (*Perrin*, 1988).

Specialty costing

Interest in extending cost analysis down to the level of the clinician (the ultimate decision-maker on the use of NHS resources) was promulgated in the 1970s (*Hillman and Nix*, 1982). Professor Magee of University College, Cardiff, was commissioned by the DHSS to develop an inexpensive system of costing for specialties, i.e. determining the average cost of treating patients within clinical specialties (general surgery, paediatrics, etc.). The original field trials relied on uncomputerised data from service departments (laboratories, pharmacy, radiology, etc.) and sampling was used to form a basis for cost apportionments.

Specialty costs have also been compiled using regression analysis (*Ashford and Cumming*, 1991). Multiple regression techniques were applied to the data held centrally by the DHSS (hospital costs and bed-use data) to determine the statistical average cost of some 40 clinical specialties. The specialty costs determined by this technique were used in the 1980s to adjust the financial allocation targets of regional and district health authorities for flows of patients across administrative boundaries.

However, it was not until 1984 that specialty costing as a minimum for all health authorities was recommended (*DHSS*, 1984). Specialty cost returns formed part of annual reporting from 1987. Specialty costing returns provided by many DHAs were not compiled as part of a continuous specialty costing system: apportionments were frequently based on sample data and were carried out only annually. The specialty costs only applied to 'direct patient care services' rather than total hospital costs. Specialty cost returns were the lowest level of cost information which health authorities were required to provide in 1989. The costs were only required to be produced for each DHA rather than each hospital and were not included in performance indicators published by the Department of Health. Nevertheless, there were a number of national and local initiatives providing more detailed information at individual hospitals.

Regional and supra-regional specialties

The funding of regional and supra-regional specialty work has often required the hospitals where such work is undertaken to examine the costs more thoroughly than in statutory specialty costing returns. Regional specialty sites were required to compile procedure prices for some regional specialty work in the years prior to the reforms. For example, in the West Midlands Region, a procedure profile was required for bone marrow transplantation.

The profile includes:

specific drugs
specific medical and surgical items
theatre usage
in-patient bed days

out-patient clinic attendances
X-ray requests
pathology requests
para-medic contacts
EEG/ ECG requests

The costing method divides costs into five categories: direct consumables (drugs, theatre, etc.); bed day cost per ward (nursing, medical, catering, laundry, linen, non-specific medical supplies); out-patient clinic costs; other patient treatment services; and overheads. The method of assigning other patient treatment services is prescribed (e.g. weighted requests for radiology), as is the method of assigning overheads 'in order to ensure consistency across sites, and for simplicity of application the chosen method allocates overheads on the basis of in-patient days and weighted out-patient attendances' (*WMRHA Regional Specialty Services, Costing Manual, 1988/89*).

Resource management and other initiatives

Impetus was given to clinical management budgets by the Griffiths Inquiry Report, but development work on clinical budgeting had been pioneered earlier by CASPE and local initiatives.

Management budgeting

In 1983, four demonstration districts for management budgets were set up and two firms of management consultants were appointed to assist in the development. Management budgets were to involve clinicians and relate service and workload objectives to financial and manpower allocations. The aim was to shift the focus of cost accountability from the person responsible for the initial expenditure (head of pathology, pharmacy, etc.) to the clinician responsible for their consumption. All service costs and overheads were to be included and standard costing techniques were to be employed.

Resource management initiatives (RMI)

In 1986, RMIs were developed from the former management budgeting exercises:

> *'to enable the National Health Service to give better service to its patients, by helping clinicians and other managers to make better informed judgements about how the resources they control can be used to maximum effect.'* *DHSS* (1986)

RMI is a wider, more participative concept than management budgeting. The demonstration sites had failed because of either a lack of commitment from the majority of clinical staff or inadequate computer support (*Perrin*, 1988). To overcome these problems, RMI was to be centred around developing and using information which doctors and nurses themselves think will help them better to organise and manage their work rather than the mechanics of information and accounting systems. The principal aim is to demonstrate whether the new approach to resource management results in measurable improvements in patient care.

The information required to support the RMI is known as the 'case-mix management system'. The basis of the system is the individual patient record including all events occurring to the patient. Operational data is fed from either a single feeder system (i.e. an integrated system) or from a number of feeder systems (*NHS Management Board*, 1989). The integrated systems are known as Hospital Information Support Systems (HISS). Each event occurring during the patient's episode of treatment is costed using standard costs defined for each hospital. In the years prior to the reforms, the RMI sites had been developing the use of diagnostic-related groups (DRGs) as a means of grouping patients for meaningful analysis.

When the NHS reforms were announced, it was widely believed that the six RM pilot sites initiated in 1986 would provide the answer to hospitals' information needs and enable them to generate sufficiently reliable cost information to operate treatment tariffs, and enter into commercial contracts with DHAs, GPFHs or other purchasers. Consequently, further hospitals were chosen as RM 'roll out' sites to pilot systems which could be extended to all 260 major acute hospitals in the country.

However, in 1989, the original RMI sites had much development work to undertake to achieve their objectives (objectives conceived before the major changes outlined in 'Working for Patients'). The Central Consultants and Specialists Committee (CCSC) of the BMA was concerned about the extension of the initiative before their plans to evaluate the sites, and in their October 1989 evaluation stated that:

> *'whilst encouraged by the experience of the experimental sites, the CCSC is not yet convinced that the evidence so far justifies extending RMI to additional sites.'* *CCSC* (1989)

Furthermore, the interim report of the Brunel University Evaluation Team pointed out the dearth of financial information and the lack of a consistent approach to its collection:

> *'Initially most sites concentrated on the collection of activity data, and not so much on the development of financial systems: this was a conscious decision on their part. However, the sites have been working on methods of costing individual patient episodes. Some have based their approach on the use of standard costs, others are seeking to use a combination of actual and standard costs. There is no overall agreement at present on the approaches to costing.'*
>
> *Buxton et al.* (1989)

In 1990, a brief review of the RM sites was undertaken to assess their contribution to future costing and pricing of healthcare contracts in the NHS internal market (*Ellwood*, 1992). As the focus of RM had been on involving doctors and nurses in managing their resources, the greater part of the hospital budgets at the RM hospitals was attributed to clinical directorates. The extent of delegation to clinical directorates varied between RM hospitals: at Guy's Hospital 67 per cent of hospital expenditure was attributed to directorates; at Huddersfield Royal Infirmary all expenditure was attributed to directorates. The RM hospitals had invested heavily in computer systems, including case-mix management systems. Indeed, all the RM hospitals, except one which had still to incur its main programme of computer implementation, made over £1m investment in information systems between starting RM and the end of 1990. While the hospitals had been experimenting with the use of DRGs, they did not use DRGs or any other form of patient grouping as part of routine management. Care profiles consisting of the expected pattern of care for a given type of patient were also being developed at the RM hospitals.

Although one of the original aims of RM expressed by the Department of Health and Social Security was to develop case-mix planning and costing (*DHSS*, 1986), most RM hospitals had been slow to introduce costs into the RM database. Huddersfield Royal Infirmary was regarded as one of the most advanced in 1989 (*Ellwood*, 1992). Standard costs were held in the case-mix system for the following events: ward cost per day; pathology test; radiology investigation; therapy recorded unit; drugs; theatre time. None of the RM hospitals had been able to provide budgets based on standard costs and expressed in terms of case-mix activity by consultant/ specialty.

Local initiatives

In addition to the major changes or initiatives instigated by the DoH which are considered below, a number of further projects had been undertaken locally. For example, the Financial Information Project (FIP) originally based at West Midlands RHA had been developing patient costing using a modular approach (ward nursing; operating theatres, etc.). Local district initiatives included the Bradford–Calderdale computer system for compiling annual specialty cost returns and the Medical Activity Resource System (MARS) at Central Birmingham HA for producing reports by clinicians. A small number of districts operated computer models to simulate the effect of changing activity levels on hospital costs.

Departmental costing systems

Many hospitals had developed costing systems as part of a service department's operational system. These costing systems are useful in informing clinicians of their resource usage and encouraging efficient practices. They also enable specialty cost statements to be compiled more accurately. The departmental cost systems can be constructed very simply by using crude workload measures or, preferably, using relative value units (RVUs) or (engineered) standard costs. For example, a haematology laboratory may use merely the number of requests received for investigations as the cost object, it may use the Welcan system which weights individual work performed according to the staff time required for each investigation, or it may compile the standard cost of each investigation by monitoring the quantity and cost of each resource consumed. Departmental cost systems are only as good as the costs which are fed into them, and quite distorted resource-use information can be provided if inadequate workload measures are used. For example, the cost of a GP fundholder's work using a simple unweighted request as the workload measure at a hospital laboratory may be considerably more than if the work is costed according to the type of investigation requested, as the GP fundholder generally requests much simpler investigations than the hospital clinicians.

Cost demonstration sites 1990

The lowest level of analysis for most DHAs in 1990 was the specialty cost information provided in the financial return FR12. This analysis was not based on the total hospital costs and it was undertaken often with dubious precision. In 1990 the Department of Health established ten cost demonstration sites 'to apply the cost allocation principles proposed by the Department of Health across the range of contracts envisaged by a provider unit.'

The pilot sites established the total cost to be recovered from a variety of sources: four started from budget data while the remainder worked from historical costs. The sites starting the exercise from historical costs generally started from FR12 data (i.e. existing specialty costs for direct treatment services), but the remainder either started from basic general ledger data or FR11 departmental cost data (*Ellwood*, 1992). Starting from the FR12 largely pre-empts the use of departmental overhead absorption; although obviously quicker and simpler to use, this approach is likely to be less satisfactory in measuring the resource use of the specialties. Although historical data enables relatively easy reconciliation of prices with costs, which is necessary for audit purposes, the costs must be uplifted, adjusted for any non-recurring items and developments and any budget under/overspends.

All but one of the demonstration sites envisaged costing the majority of their contracts on a specialty basis with apportioned hospital indirect and overhead costs, though costing for a small number of procedures was undertaken at some sites. However, many expressed their future commitment to a procedure costing system.

Harefield Hospital used a procedure cost approach whereby 20 per cent of the hospital's expenditure was related directly to procedure cost centres and the rest was identified to variable or fixed pools for each specialty and then absorbed into procedures (or grouped procedures). Thus some bottom-up costing was undertaken for direct treatment costs (e.g. theatres) while indirect expenditure was allocated and apportioned to specialties for absorption into procedures. The top-down cost mapping employed by the sites varied considerably. Some pilots (e.g. Scunthorpe) used a staged approach, i.e. determining full departmental/subjective expenditure head cost and attributing to facilities, community or external contracts and then attributing each facility or service cost to specialties. Others appear to have apportioned individual cost heads directly to specialties on whatever basis was appropriate and available.

Cost behaviour was not examined rigorously by the sites though some sites analysed elements of cost into fixed and variable categories. A mixture of definitions was used and analysis was generally very limited; some stated no work to date. The NHSME formally concluded from the work of the cost demonstration sites that:

> *'average specialty costs can be calculated prospectively on a full-cost basis for contract pricing purposes using existing information systems.'*
>
> *NHSME* (1990c)

However, the fact that hospitals are able to arrive at a full specialty cost is not really the issue, and indeed such costs could have been achieved very simplistically by a percentage addition to the FR12 cost returns. The difficulty is in using these costs for prices in an internal market. They are unlikely to provide appropriate signals to guide purchasers: inadequate product definition, poor workload measures and inconsistent treatment of overheads will impede valid comparisons between hospitals.

5.4 Hospital cost accounting in the USA

Hospital cost accounting methods

Given the comparatively strong market approach to healthcare provision and purchasing in the USA, it would appear reasonable to expect US hospitals to employ cost systems which clearly establish the cost of healthcare 'products'. In 1990 some hospitals in the USA had cost accounting systems which employed a standard costing approach integrated into an overall resource management context. Industrial model systems are not the norm, though their incidence is increasing (*HFMA Massachusetts*, 1991; *Counte and Glandon*, 1988), or as advanced as their literature suggests (*Orloff et al.*, 1990). In 1989 a survey of 89 Massachusetts hospitals found that only 29 hospitals (30 per cent) had computerised costing systems and that ten of these hospitals reported not currently using the systems (*HFMA Massachusetts*, 1989). A much larger survey of 3000 acute care hospitals, carried out by Price Waterhouse in 1985, found that 1533 had some type of computerised cost accounting system, but hospitals with fewer than 100 beds were not included. Most hospitals impute patient costs from patient charges, the ratio of costs to charges (RCC) method. The Massachusetts survey found that 61 per cent of acute hospitals used the RCC method to determine costs by DRG.

The RCC method calculates for each charge centre (e.g. X-ray) the ratio of the total cost to the total charges; a consistent relationship between total charges and total costs is then assumed for all the work of the department. For example, if the RCC for the X-ray department is 70 per cent, this would be applied to charges for individual X-rays to deduce the cost of each type of X-ray. Such costings are highly inaccurate, and there is often no relationship between costs and charges (*Schimmel et al.*, 1987; *McFadden*, 1990), a point which has also been noted with regard to private hospitals in the UK. RCCs result from the Medicare cost report process. In compiling these, hospitals will have aimed to maximise reimbursement rather than focus on accurately attributing costs. Those hospitals that were most adept at maximising reimbursement through rate setting will tend to have particularly distorted cost information.

On the other hand, there are some isolated examples of cost accounting systems operating along business principles and integrated with the resource management approach such as at the New England Medical Center (NEMC) in Boston (*Elkwood*, 1992). The NEMC developed and maintained a sophisticated cost accounting system throughout the 1980s and subsequently introduced the system into many other hospitals in the USA. The costing model shown in Figure 5.2 uses business principles commonly applied in industry, e.g. responsibility centres, marginal costing, standard costing, variance analysis and sales forecasting.

Figure 5.2: The costing model – New England Medical Center

Hospital production function	Raw goods Labour, supplies, capital	Intermediate products Nursing, lab tests, X-rays	End products DRG ICD-9-CM Surgery procedures	Product lines HMO/PPO Specialty services
Type/level management	Departmental		Clinical	Finance/planning/ marketing
Managerial objectives	Manage the cost of raw goods and services	Manage the unit cost of intermediate products	Manage the utilisation of intermediate products	Market existing products to new markets Market new products to existing markets Improve bottom line

The focus is on the control and management of costs of intermediate products. This embodies: identification of fixed and variable costs within each department; definition of intermediate products for subsequent costing; development of standard unit costs, indirect cost allocation/apportionment; variance analysis and department cost simulation. NEMC is able to use the costings of intermediate products together with defined treatment protocols to establish budgets. The treatment protocols delineate the appropriate range in number and mix of services necessary for providing care to a very specifically defined (homogeneous) type of patient. Comparison of actual and budgeted resource use can therefore enable meaningful variance analysis. Although standards are used for all patient-level details, therapy departments are often based on relative value units or included in indirect overhead. The '80/20' rule is often applied: each service item is ranked by budgeted $ volume; the 20 per cent of the service items that are expected to account for 80 per cent of the $ volume receive the majority of the costing attention; the remaining 80 per cent of service items representing 20 per cent of the $ volume are costed in a less time-consuming manner. Furthermore, the costs held on patient records are uplifted by 20 to 25 per cent to cover general overheads. No significant benefit is perceived to justify the development of complicated methods for attributing remote overheads to patients. NEMC sees its cost accounting system as increasingly important in ensuring the negotiation of viable contracts with health maintenance organisations (HMOs) and preferred provider organisations (PPOs) and also in assessing the true return on work undertaken under Medicare DRG reimbursement.

Wise (1992) emphasises that there are marked differences between the purpose of cost accounting in the USA and in the NHS internal market. In the UK, the prices are to be based on cost for contracting purposes. If costs are 'incorrect', contracting decisions are made on an erroneous basis and providers achieve unplanned under- or over-recovery of costs. In the USA, the role of cost accounting is to *compare* costs with reimbursement rates (charges or, for Medicare patients, a fixed price per DRG); costs do not determine price. If costs are 'incorrect' management information on product profitability is misleading. In the USA competition in healthcare is usually non-price competition as the consumer is generally insured and is therefore not paying the hospital directly. Consequently, the consumer has little incentive to make cost-efficient choices. However, cost sharing arrangements have been extended in recent years and the HMOs and PPOs have taken an increasing share of the traditional insurance and fee-for-service market.

Health maintenance organisations and selective contracting

Health maintenance organisations have grown dramatically over the last 20 years. In 1970 there were fewer than 30 serving just under 3 million people, whereas by 1988 there were over 700 catering for over 29 million people (*Stoline and Weiner*, 1988). A typical HMO operates through patients paying a set annual fee, usually through their employer. In return the HMO contracts to provide all the necessary healthcare. Healthcare may be delivered through a staff model HMO, such as Kaiser Permanente, in which doctors are employed directly on a salaried basis; or a group model HMO in which a large group practice provides care; or with a number of practices (a network model); or with a number of solo practitioners or small groups.

Preferred provider organisations are insurance plans which offer more choice between doctors than the HMO model but not complete freedom as under traditional indemnity schemes. PPOs negotiate fee-for-service discounts with specified doctors and hospitals in return for an anticipated volume of work, thus enabling lower premiums to enrolees. PPOs have expanded rapidly since 1983 and now cover as many enrolees as HMOs.

The Kaiser Permanente is the largest HMO. It receives monies to provide healthcare to its members, usually through its own directly managed hospitals, but it also places contracts with 'outside' hospitals for the care of some of its members. Thus there appears an obvious similarity to the position of DHAs on the introduction of the internal market, responsible for purchasing care for their population and providing care through their own directly managed NHS hospitals. The Kaiser Foundation Hospitals provide the hospital services required by health plan members and Medicare recipients. The nature of the service provision is loosely defined in hospital service agreements. Although the Kaiser organisation provides most of the healthcare requirements of its members internally, contracts are placed with outside hospitals under two circumstances. Firstly, some procedures are very specialist and it would be uneconomic or unfeasible for Kaiser hospitals to provide appropriate care, e.g. bone marrow transplants. Secondly, there may be a lack of capacity in some locations; this is particularly the case in the San Diego area where the population is expanding rapidly.

When contracts are placed for very specialist procedures, the content and cost is clearly broken down in the contract; for example, transplants would be broken down into three stages prior to transfer to Kaiser direct provision: evaluation; surgery; follow-up care. For each stage the resources and cost would be clearly set out, as shown in Appendix 1 for liver transplants.

Where there is a lack of capacity in Kaiser hospitals a contract may be placed with an outside hospital, sometimes through a tender system. These contracts are often placed on a *per diem* basis and therefore an outside utilisation programme employing public health nurses and physician advisors is necessary. Staff are located on site, they review charts and issue notice of non-coverage if appropriate. Discharge planning, transfers to follow-up care, bill processing, quality assurance services and repatriation of members to the Kaiser system are facilitated by the review staff.

5.5 *Summary*

The cost information available in the NHS had developed rapidly in the years prior to the reforms. However, there was still very little information available at the level required for costing and pricing healthcare contracts, especially cost and volume and cost per case work. Standard costing was rare and still in its infancy. In 1990, the lowest level of cost information generally available to hospitals was the FR12 specialty cost return, which included only direct patient care costs. The cost demonstration sites had largely derived full-cost specialty prices. However, such cost-based prices were unlikely to provide appropriate signals to guide purchasers. The resource management sites and the cost methods adopted at some US hospitals indicate potential approaches for achieving meaningful cost-based prices. Further lessons from the USA are that in the NHS internal market contracts for expensive, high-technology medicine provided by outside hospitals will require very detailed specification and pricing. It is extremely difficult to ensure quality and efficiency through contract specification alone. Purchasers may require utilisation management and audit programmes to supplement contracts.

The methods actually adopted by NHS hospitals in the first year of the NHS internal market are considered in the next chapter.

6 The 1991 West Midlands Survey of Cost-based Prices

6.1 Introduction

This chapter considers the prices used for contracts in 1991/92 and the cost methods on which they were based. A database of prices quoted by acute hospitals in the West Midlands Region (the largest of the fourteen health regions in England) was compiled. In order to assess the basis of the prices, a questionnaire on the costing methods used was distributed to acute hospitals in the region. The questionnaire also included questions on the market environment, the form of contracts, information systems and contract categories (i.e. product groupings). Conclusions are drawn as to the reliability of 1991/92 pricing methods as a means of allocating health service resources in an internal market, and how it was envisaged that cost-based pricing would develop is set out.

6.2 The contract pricing arrangements for 1991/92

In order to achieve 'a smooth takeoff' of the internal market, the operation of the market was strongly controlled in 1991/92. The basic principles for pricing were set by the NHSME:

> *'Provider units will need to price their services so that the income recovered matches the net costs incurred. There are three fundamental principles underlying the way in which service costs and prices are to be established:*

> *a. prices should be based on costs;*
> *b. costs should generally be arrived at on a full cost basis;*
> *c. there should be no planned cross-subsidisation between contracts.*
>
> *... The guidance permits a large degree of discretion to units in the detailed methods they adopt for cost allocation, and apportionment, but the methods should in all cases conform to these principles.'*
> *NHSME* (1990a)

The NHSME claimed that an initial solution would be to set prices on an average specialty cost basis using the Korner costs and activity returns. Although contracts would be negotiated mainly at specialty level for DHAs, each hospital had to produce prices at clinical procedure level for GPFHs as 113 hospital procedures were to be included in GPFH budgets. The GPFH procedure-level contracts were regarded as requiring extra precision.

> *'One way of determining costs might be for providers to use average specialty costs as a starting point and to adjust for significant differences between procedures in operating time, consumables and length of stay. Procedures with similar resource use could then be banded.'* *NHSME* (1990a)

The internal market was severely restricted in its first year of operation.

> *'For 1991/92 there is a strong presumption in favour of block contracts for major patient flows.'* *NHSME* (1990b)

The NHSME went on to explain in a later document that dramatic changes in activity would be likely to disrupt patient services, so that service specification in 1991/92 would need to describe activity based on the current pattern of services, except where planned changes had been agreed with providers (*NHSME*, 1991). The first year's contracting was largely about developing the mechanics of the contracting system. The contracts were to be largely block contracts at specialty level and, for DHAs, were to reflect existing referral patterns. The market was not to be able to respond to price and quantity signals. However, if the benefits of a market approach were to be fully realised through a more efficient allocation of the limited NHS resources, such impediments would have to be removed in later years.

6.3 1991/92 prices in the West Midlands

A database of GPFH procedure prices and ECR (extra-contractual referral) prices throughout the West Midlands Region was compiled. Hospitals were instructed that ECR prices should be constructed on the same basis as mainstream contracts, and therefore ECR prices should be indicative of contract prices.

The database revealed vast variations in the specialty prices, as shown in Table 6.1. Depending on which hospital in the region is selected, a consultant episode can cost from £350 to £1353 in obstetrics and from £469 to £3417 in dermatology and so on. For the internal market to operate satisfactorily price differentials between NHS providers must be indicative of efficiency and/or quality. However, the choice of clinical specialty as the cost product is bound to give rise to distortions due to differences in case mix or complexity between hospitals. Specialty costs are generally believed to be at too high a level of aggregation of clinical work to be meaningful as resource groups. Product groupings are discussed in section 4.3. The USA and many European and Scandinavian countries prefer to use diagnostic-related groups (DRGs), as indeed has the NHS in its resource management approach, to classify patients into types that are similar both clinically and in the resources they use.

Table 6.1: Specialty prices 1991/92 – West Midlands acute hospitals

Specialty	Price per consultant episode			Coefficient of variation
	Average £	*High £*	*Low £*	%
General medicine	1,160	1,472	923	14
Paediatrics	767	1,139	371	27
Dermatology	1,830	3,417	469	59
General surgery	1,148	1,477	713	16
Urology	985	1,714	595	30
Orthopaedics	1,493	2,311	854	23
ENT	754	1,203	457	27
Ophthalmology	934	1,483	518	27
Gynaecology	635	915	443	22
Obstetrics	761	1,353	350	36

It was therefore expected that less variation would be found in procedure costs which are broadly in line with DRGs (Table 6.2).

However, the variation in prices of many procedures between hospitals, as measured by the coefficient of variation, is greater than the variation between specialty prices per episode. The prices quoted by NHS hospitals in the West Midlands were generally below those for fixed-price surgery in private hospitals. For example, BUPA quoted a price of £1097 and £1895 for varicose veins (unilateral and bilateral respectively); this compared with an average of £544 in NHS hospitals in the West Midlands with a range of £287 to £1278. The fundamental question is whether these prices are adequate for the market mechanism to operate effectively. Does the 1991/92 price for treatment of an ingrowing toenail at one West Midlands hospital of £91 compared with £656 at another provide the right signals to the market?

Table 6.2: Procedure prices 1991/92 – West Midlands acute hospitals

Procedure[1]	Price per consultant episode			Range	Coefficient of variation
	Average £	*High £*	*Low £*	£	%
Total colectomy	2,722	4,968	958	4,010	27
Varicose veins	544	1,278	287	991	38
Ingrowing toenail	236	656	91	565	44
Skin biopsy	363	1,165	91	1,074	64
Lymph node excision	518	958	213	745	34

1 The above general surgery procedure prices were selected from 113 published procedure prices within the specialties of ophthalmology, ENT, general surgery, urology, gynaecology and orthopaedics.

In the internal market, the price mechanism is to replace the previous resource allocation system which provided global budgets to hospitals. Price variations are an important facet of a market system; the market will only improve resource allocation if prices fairly reflect costs. Such price variations in procedures could be due to the crude nature of the costing approaches rather than true variations in treatment patterns and the cost of resource inputs. At first glance, the pricing structures used were sometimes crude. For example, one eminent hospital used only two prices for the 91 GPFH procedures which it provided, £958 and £303. This hospital had the highest price in the region for nineteen procedures and the lowest price for eleven procedures. In order to assess the reliability of the prices in more depth, the questionnaire sent to acute hospitals in the West Midlands covered the approach to costing contracts/ECRs and GPFH procedures.

6.4 *The questionnaire survey*

The questionnaire asked for factual data concerning the types of contracts, the number of purchasers, how the costs were compiled for pricing purposes and the activity information systems. Two 'opinion' questions were included regarding factors likely to have led to abnormal costs and the hospital's future costing and pricing strategy. The questionnaire was sent to the accountants responsible for 'costing for contracting' at 49 acute hospitals in the region (listed earlier in Table 1.1). Replies were received from 36 hospitals, a response rate of 74 per cent.

The hospitals which responded ranged from small community and eye hospitals with budgets under £5m to large teaching hospitals with budgets over £50m (Figure 6.1a). The total expenditure of hospitals in the survey was £853m in 1991. Although ten (27 per cent) hospitals had budgets below £10m (Figure 6.1b) these small hospitals accounted for only 6 per cent of expenditure (Figure 6.1c).

Figure 6.1a: The expenditure of the hospitals in the survey

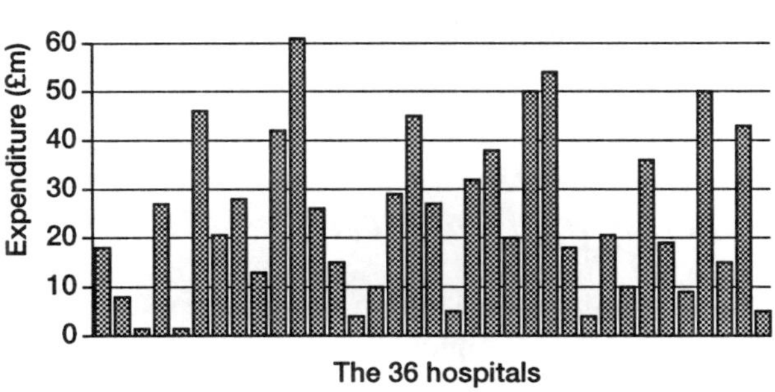

Figure 6.1b: Hospitals in the survey analysed by size £

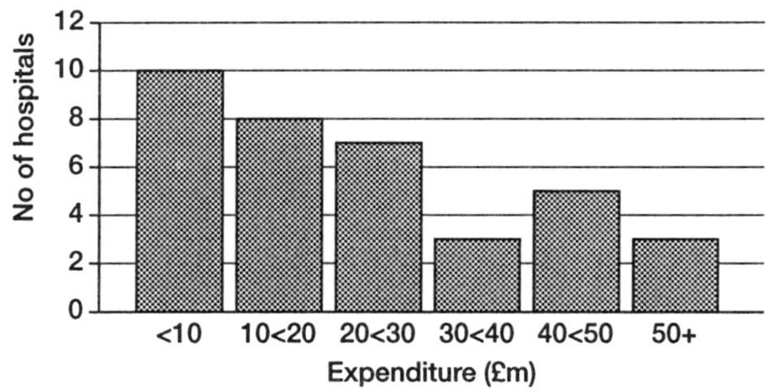

Figure 6.1c: Total service expenditure by hospital size

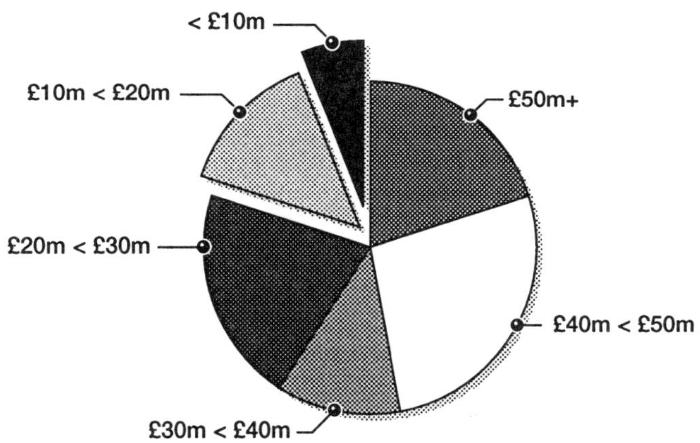

The market in the West Midlands

The questionnaire results showed the nature of the market to be very diverse. Of the 36 hospitals completing the questionnaire the contracting environment varied from one hospital with contracts with only two health authorities (Princess Royal in Shropshire) to one holding contracts with 23 health authorities (Queen Elizabeth, Birmingham). The Birmingham hospitals faced considerably more competition than the other hospitals, and seven of the eight hospitals which contracted with fifteen or more DHAs were within the city. Similarly, the number of contracts with GPFHs varied from nil to sixteen at Birmingham Women's Hospital. The average provider hospital contracted with ten health authorities and two GPFHs.

However, a third of hospitals contracted with six or fewer DHAs and could be regarded as experiencing monopsony power.

A research study by the National Association of Health Authorities and Trusts (NAHAT) monitoring the degree of competition in general surgery faced by hospitals in the West Midlands Region suggested that in 1988 only a quarter of them operated in markets where the degree of competition was such that elements of monopoly or oligopoly power might exist (*Robinson,* 1991). The NAHAT study employed the Hirschman–Herfindahl index; the approach is explained below. In the USA, the Department of Justice uses the index to assess anti-trust cases; the index ranges from 0 – perfect competition – to 10,000 – total monopoly. Firms with values in excess of 1800 are considered to be in potentially monopolistic positions (*Melnick and Zwanziger*, 1988). The NAHAT study constructed the index for 39 West Midlands acute hospitals using patient-flow data for one particular specialty, general surgery. This involved three main stages: identification of each hospital's market area; identification of each hospital's competitors within each market area; and production of an overall index of competition for each hospital, based upon the number of competitors in its market area(s) and their market shares. Applying the Department of Justice's cut-off point to the West Midlands hospitals suggests that in 1991 a third were in monopoly positions. If attention is focused on the number of patients treated by these hospitals, rather than simply the hospitals themselves, the degree of concentration becomes somewhat higher (*Appleby et al.*, 1994).

Consequently, it appears that for acute health care in the West Midlands Health Region a significant level of monopsony and monopoly power exists. Contestable market proponents would argue that it is potential competitors rather than merely existing competitors that ensure that existing 'firms' operate efficiently, but in hospital provision significant barriers to new entrants exist (*Robinson,* 1990). The transaction costs line of argument (because contracts are expensive to write, complicated to execute and difficult to enforce) suggests the desirability of long-term stable contractual relationships between purchasers and providers.

The form of the contracts held also showed extreme diversity. The average provider hospital had the pattern of contract income shown in Table 6.3. However, seven hospitals earned all of their contract income through block (with and without indicative volume) contracts, while at the other extreme one hospital earned 95 per cent of its contract income through cost and volume contracts and 5 per cent of income through cost per case; another hospital earned 100 per cent through cost and volume contracts.

Table 6.3: 1991/92 contract income by type of contract

Type of contract	% of contract income
Block	30
Block with indicative volume	58
Cost and volume	9
Cost per case	3
TOTAL (survey respondents)	100

Block contracts which are specified in terms of facilities to be provided are similar to previous NHS management practice. Under a block contract, a provider is paid an annual sum in instalments in return for access for the purchaser's resident population to a defined range of services (*DoH*, 1989c). Block contracts specify resources in terms of beds or doctors, linked to particular specialties. Such contracts are low risk for the provider as the DHA provides resources in regular instalments, irrespective of the volume of patients treated, and for which no explicit usage is prescribed. However, there is little incentive to improve efficiency; indeed, the efficiency trap remains – reports of hospitals running out of funds and taking only emergency patients were still common at the end of the first year of the NHS internal market. The purchaser has little control, and crucial decisions about the volume and nature of outputs to be produced stay on the provider side.

Cost and volume contracts place an explicit requirement on the provider in terms of patients treated. Often a fixed price is paid up to a volume threshold above which a price per case is set up to a volume ceiling. Such contracts are more risky for the provider (though obviously more satisfactory from the purchaser perspective).

Cost per case contracts are obviously the most risky, the provider would have no certainty of income, while the purchaser would risk losing control of its expenditure if it were to incur large commitments on a per case basis. It is fundamental to the efficiency of market price mechanisms that quantity of provision is considered in relation to price. Consequently, if incentives to technical efficiency are to be provided, contracting must move away from block contracts to contracts which clearly relate price to quantity of *output.*

In order to investigate the financial vulnerability of hospitals in the first year of the market, the hospitals were asked to categorise their income into three elements:

- fixed (block contracts and the floor level of cost and volume contracts);
- variable (cost per case contracts – ECRs, private patients);
- non-patient care (special funds for training, etc.).

In 1991/92, only two hospitals had more than 5 per cent of their income classified as variable. However, given the fixed nature of most hospital costs even small percentage falls in funding can have dramatic effects. Twelve hospitals classified between 2 and 4 per cent of their income as variable.

The position of hospitals in the internal market in the West Midlands is diverse. It poses much more of a threat or opportunity to some hospitals than others, and consequently the importance of realistic pricing and costing methods is much greater to the more market-oriented hospitals.

6.5 The cost methods behind the prices

In costing and pricing contracts for health authorities, all 36 hospitals used a specialty cost approach, although GPFH contracts and regional specialty contracts were priced at a more detailed level. Most hospitals (22, or 61 per cent) used the annual financial return FR12 specialty costs as the start point, a further four used actual financial ledger costs fed into the in-house Medical Activity Resource System (MARS), and eleven used budget information.

The classification of costs by expenditure type by the 36 hospitals surveyed is shown in Table 6.4. However, considerable variation was apparent: one hospital classified only 43 per cent of its costs as direct patient treatment while another classified 68 per cent as direct patient treatment; capital charges varied from as little as 4 per cent to over 20 per cent of total costs!

Table 6.4: Classification by expenditure type – West Midlands acute hospitals

Cost classification of the average hospital	%
Direct patient treatment	61
General services	20
DHQ	3
RHA	2
Capital	14

Capital charges

The capital charging system introduced into the NHS is complex. The basic idea is that capital charges are made up of a current cost depreciation charge plus 6 per cent interest. The system is explained more fully in Appendix 2. The findings of the survey are in line with those of a Department of Health survey of 146 districts, where 80 per cent of districts estimated that the costs arising from capital charges would represent between 10 per cent and 20 per cent of their revenue allocations, although one inner London district put the figure as high as 39 per cent. Considerable difficulties were encountered in applying capital charges in the NHS in 1991 (the first year of capital accounting). Massive discrepancies in the estimates of capital charges across the country forced the Department of Health to effectively 'write off the first year of the system as a purely paper exercise' (*Health Service Journal*, 5 December 1991). Estimated figures for 1991/92 produced in October 1990 by one district in the West Midlands were almost £2m or 33 per cent above the revised/actual charges for 1991/92. The NHS had enormous teething problems in moving from a system where the principles of capital accounting were entirely absent to one in which all assets over £1000 needed to have interest and current cost depreciation applied. The limit was subsequently raised to £5000. Further difficulties concerned the leaking of funds to the private sector (when DHAs and GPFHs placed contracts with private organisations) and the treatment of providers in areas with high property and land costs (*NAHAT*, 1991). From the point of view of economic efficiency, it is important that the costs of capital items are not ignored, but its value in representing opportunity cost in 1991/92 is extremely limited.

Treatment of overheads

For the average hospital, non-direct patient care services account for 39 per cent of total costs (Table 6.4). Therefore a large proportion of healthcare costs cannot be directly attributed to contracts. The vast majority of hospitals included such costs by an addition to in-patient and out-patient contracts rather than through a staged (step-down) approach, i.e. assigning to direct treatment departments such as theatres, radiology, etc., for absorption into specialties. Figure 6.2 illustrates the extent to which selected support service costs were assigned to patient treatment departments for absorption into contracts.

Figure 6.2: Assignment of support service costs

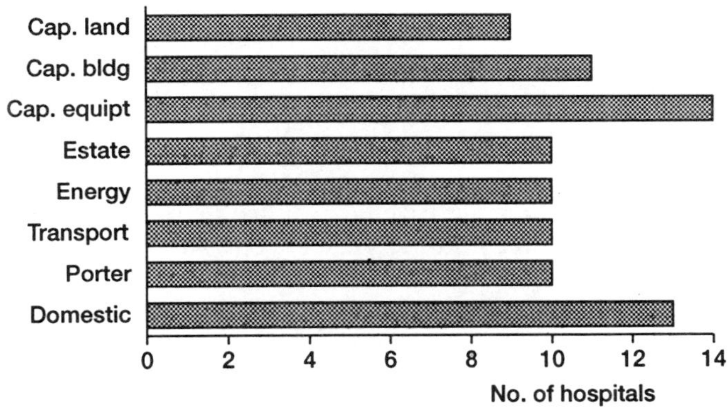

Note: Three hospitals had only assigned part of domestic service costs, and capital charges (three groups) to patient treatment areas.

For some remote overheads this may be acceptable, but less than a third of hospitals fully assigned capital equipment to treatment departments; given the heavy capital equipment costs in some treatment departments (e.g. radiology) this must have distorted specialty costs.

Direct patient treatment services

The problem of achieving reasonable specialty costs and hence, realistic prices was further exacerbated by the limited availability of activity/cost systems for direct patient treatment services. None of the 36 hospitals had a case-mix management system and departmental costing systems were quite rare, as shown in Table 6.5. Case-mix management systems enable resource use to be recorded against individual patient records and analysed by patient characteristic. Without such systems reliable costing below specialty level will be difficult to achieve. Even at specialty level, in 1991/92 not only were overheads treated crudely, but also many direct patient care costs were assigned to contracts based on very limited financial information owing to the lack of departmental activity/cost systems in patient treatment departments.

Table 6.5: Operational computer systems 1991

Computer system	% of providers
Case mix	0
Nursing dependency	17
Pharmacy	42
Theatre	17
Pathology	36
Radiology	22

Many hospitals stated that departmental cost systems were being introduced: a further nine hospitals (25 per cent) were installing nursing cost management systems; a further six (17 per cent) theatre costing systems and a further five (14 per cent) pharmacy costing systems. However, departmental cost systems for attributing direct patient care costs to contracts were not available in the majority of hospitals in 1991.

The product level

Although specialty contracts were prescribed as the norm for hospitals in 1991, hospitals were required to produce prices at procedure level for GPFHs. Most hospitals had limited information from which to compile such prices. All hospitals based the procedure prices on specialty in-patient day costs. These were modified by 56 per cent of hospitals for prostheses, by 47 per cent for theatre costs and by 17 per cent for drug costs. Over 30 per cent of hospitals made no adjustments to the specialty in-patient day cost when compiling procedure costs. The variable costs relating to prostheses, drugs and theatre usage are likely to be significantly different from the average specialty cost for some GPFH procedures. For example, in the orthopaedic specialty, GPFH procedures include 'lumbar injection' and 'implanted bone substance', both of which had price variations in the West Midlands Region with coefficients of variation above 50 per cent. Rather than setting individual prices for all 113 procedures, six hospitals (or 17 per cent) banded the procedures for pricing purposes; a common structure was major, intermediate and minor for each specialty, but there was not necessarily any common agreement as to which procedures fell into each grouping.

In determining their hospital costs and prices, 33 hospitals (92 per cent) had used linked spreadsheets designed in-house or by another DHA and four had used the MARS model based on FCS software. Changes in expected activity levels had often been treated crudely; some stated 'general percentage uplift', while only 25 per cent claimed to have made a systematic analysis of fixed and variable components.

6.6 Survey findings and implications

- Large variations in specialty prices were apparent in hospitals throughout the region; however, procedure prices were even more diverse. It is extremely unlikely that such variations were largely due to different treatment patterns, efficiency or quality.
- The vulnerability of hospitals to market forces varied considerably. One hospital surveyed contracted with only two DHAs while at the other extreme, one hospital held contracts with 23 DHAs.
- Nearly 90 per cent of contract income in 1991/92 was received through block contracts by acute hospitals in the West Midlands. In terms of the variability of income in 1991/92, only two hospitals had more than 5 per cent other income at risk, but a third of the survey hospitals had between 2 and 4 per cent at risk. Given the fixed nature of health service costs even modest variations can be critical. However, if prices are to lead to a more efficient distribution of NHS resources they must be clearly linked to quantity of service provided.
- Less than a third of hospitals attributed general service overheads to patient treatment departments; most attributed the overheads directly to specialties. Section 4.4 illustrates the potential discrepancies in cost attribution that can arise from such simplistic approaches.
- None of the hospitals surveyed had an operational case-mix management system, but it is difficult to see how costs can be confidently attributed below specialty level without such systems.

- Departmental cost systems were rare (e.g. only 17 per cent of hospitals had theatre costing systems), therefore even the cost attribution of some direct patient treatment services to specialties was undertaken with dubious precision. Price variances could be due to differing cost methods rather than differing efficiency.
- Over 30 per cent of the hospitals surveyed based their GPFH procedure prices entirely on specialty in-patient day costs, but there are significant variations in resource consumption over and above variations in length of stay.

Cost methods, and hence the prices produced for 1991/92 contracts and ECRs in the West Midlands, fell far short of the requirements necessary to enable an efficient allocation of NHS resources through the market. A high proportion of total costs was attributed to contracts on inadequate information. Even direct patient care costs at specialty level were of dubious credibility and the understanding of cost behaviour was very limited. Specialty contracts provided an imprecise definition of services (products) – variations in case mix within the specialty were not addressed. On the other hand, where procedure prices were compiled they were often based on inadequate data and cost methods. Prices were not a reliable indicator of resources consumed. Price differences may have been spurious; differences may have been caused by difficulties in determining the prospective quantum of cost (particularly in relation to capital charges), inadequate activity measurement and poor methods of cost attribution. Furthermore, efficiency comparisons were hampered by the lack of consistency in cost allocation and apportionment methods between different hospitals. These findings were confirmed by a CIPFA study (*CIPFA*, 1992), the Audit Commission's report and accounts for 1991/92 and the later survey undertaken by the National Steering Group on Costing.

However, in 1991/92, many restrictions were placed on the operation of the internal market: contracts were to be on the whole block contracts and for DHAs (though not necessarily GPFHs) were to reflect existing referral patterns. According to the survey, 89 per cent of hospital income was from block contracts; 8 per cent from cost and volume contracts; and 3 per cent cost per case. Block contracts which are specified in terms of facilities to be provided, and for which no explicit workload is prescribed, provide little incentive to improve efficiency. Cost and volume contracts place an explicit requirement on the provider in terms of patients treated. Often a fixed price is paid up to a volume threshold above which a price per case is set up

Figure 6.3 The internal market continuum

	1991	Mid-1990s
FORM OF CONTRACTS	Block	Cost and volume Cost per case
PRODUCT DEFINITION	Specialty	Procedure (based on grouping of treatment plans)
COST METHODS Basic approach	Top-down	Bottom-up
Direct treatment services	Few cost systems	*Departmental cost systems* Intermediate product costs • Determined by standards for all major direct treatment services • RVUs used for less significant services • Analysis of fixed and variable elements
Overheads	Allocated or apportioned according to available apportionment bases (often direct to contracts)	*Influenced by direct patient treatment* Assigned to direct patient treatment department, included in intermediate product cost. *Remote overheads* Remain at hospital level, recovered by a percentage uplift to assigned costs.
PERFORMANCE MONITORING	Limited to intermediate outputs	Systems for measuring final outcomes. Systematic Medical Audit Utilisation Review Programme.
	Departmental budgets	Budget structures based on product lines, flexed according to contracts. Variance analysis at procedure level.

Source: *Ellwood* (1992)

to a volume ceiling. Cost per case contracts are obviously the most risky, the provider has no certainty of income, while the purchaser risks losing control of expenditure if large commitments on a per case basis are incurred.

Following the survey, Figure 6.3 was developed, showing the researcher's view of how it was envisaged that contracts and cost information for pricing would progress.

6.7 Summary

This chapter has examined the cost-based pricing used in the first year of the NHS internal market. The conditions necessary for price signals to encourage economic efficiency were not apparent. Contract prices were not related to quantity, block contracts prevailed. Inadequate product definition for DHA contracts made it impossible to make valid efficiency comparisons between hospitals. Where products were more clearly defined (i.e. GPFH procedures) prices did not reflect the comparative 'true' cost of resources consumed. A high proportion of hospital costs were attributed to contracts on inadequate information and there was a lack of consistency in cost allocation and apportionment methods between hospitals. In 1991/92 cost accounting was not fulfilling its fundamental role in the NHS internal market. Improved consistency, contract categories and bases of cost attribution were required to facilitate economic efficiency. The next chapter examines how cost-based pricing in the NHS internal market had developed three years later.

7
The 1994 West Midlands Survey of Cost-based Prices

7.1 Introduction

This chapter firstly considers the detailed guidance on costing for contracting issued by the NHSME in 1993. The development of the market and costing for contracting is then investigated through the 1994 West Midlands Survey. The 1994 survey, like the 1991 survey, included a database of prices published by acute hospitals in the West Midlands and a questionnaire survey. Finally, the findings of the survey are summarised and assessed from the point of view of providing appropriate price signals within the NHS internal market.

7.2 NHSME guidance on costing for contracting

In April 1993 the NHSME issued guidance, *Costing for Contracting* (1993a). This subsequently formed the basis of the first two chapters of the *Costing for Contracting Manual* which detailed the 'minimum costing standards' to be applied in calculating prices for 1994/95 contracts.

The detailed guidance aims to:

> *'avoid differences in reported costs for the same patient treatment caused by unnecessary differences in cost allocation and apportionment between different providers'.*

The guidance establishes:

- a minimum level of identification of costs by type: direct, indirect and overhead;

- a more standardised approach to methods of apportionment for indirect costs and overheads.

Emphasis is to be placed on treating as many costs as possible as direct costs. All overheads are to be fed through patient treatment services (PTS). The movement away from 'steady state' is seen as requiring the development of a marginal costing approach and therefore the guidance also suggests:

- a minimum level of sophistication for the treatment of costs as variable, semi-fixed and fixed.

The guidance seeks to remedy some of the problems found in the 1991 survey (Chapter 6), namely the crude and inconsistent methods of cost attribution. The cost attribution methods are to require all costs to be fed through patient treatment services, whereas in 1991, assignment of support service costs to patient treatment services was patchy and *ad hoc*. The guidance also recommends minimum bases for apportionment of indirect costs (e.g. domestic services are to be apportioned according to 'floor area cleaned'). The setting out of minimum standard apportionment bases should further improve consistency and hence comparability between alternative healthcare providers.

However, the guidelines are not obligatory:

> *'The principles established represent strong guidance in the application of minimum costing standards which providers should meet as quickly as possible.'* *NHSME* (1993b)

Similarly, the distribution of costs analysed in a standard format is not obligatory. 'Voluntary co-operation' and a willingness to share cost and financial information is 'encouraged'.

The discussion on product categories in Chapter 4 and the 1991 survey (Chapter 6) highlighted the problem of identifying healthcare as a product for costing and pricing purposes. Progress on developing more meaningful product lines or contract categories is also addressed in the guidance:

> *'The National Steering Group on Costing (NSGC) believes that each specialty should be divided into a manageable number of conditions to represent treatment groupings which clinicians regard as sufficiently*

> *similar to be treated in the same way and which consume similar amounts of resource and which represent a high proportion of the total absorption costs of the specialty.'* *NHSME* (1993a)

Healthcare Resource Groups (HRGs) are to be the 'currency' used to enable a case-mix adjustment to be made to the setting and monitoring of contracts. HRGs have been developed by the National Case Mix Office. HRGs are based on DRGs, but have been modified according to British clinical practice. The proposed implementation timetable set for costing HRGs for comparison purposes was:

1 or 2 of 3 specialties	to inform 1995/96 contracts
3–11 specialties	to inform 1996/97 contracts
All specialties	to inform 1997/98 contracts.

NHSME (1993d)

From the point of view of economic efficiency, it is imperative that purchasers can compare the prices of similar products, and hence have the opportunity to respond to signals indicating relative efficiency. The introduction of suitable product groups has been tardy, but nevertheless the NHSME has set out the intended process for costing key conditions using a bottom-up analysis of costs which is reconciled to the top-down analysis prescribed in the guidance. The standard analysis of costs into overhead, indirect and direct, and the prescribed classification of costs as fixed, semi-fixed and variable, will aid comparison, but these aspects are secondary to actually identifying comparable products. Furthermore, 'openness in costing' is only 'encouraged', not obligatory, and therefore such classification and analysis may not be available to aid purchasers in their evaluation of alternative providers.

7.3 1994/95 prices in the West Midlands

To determine both how acute service providers had implemented the costing guidance and how costing for contracting was developing, a further survey of the West Midlands was undertaken. The prices of all acute DMUs and trusts were analysed. Information on average specialty prices was not available for all DMUs and trusts in the West Midlands. Many use bandings for their ECR tariffs (e.g. major, intermediate and minor), but there is no common classification for such groupings.

For 1994/95 prices, DMUs and trusts priced procedures separately for in-patient and day-case provision (Table 7.1). This has removed a large element of the variability which was present in the 1991 survey, and the coefficient of variation is 50 per cent or less for all GPFH procedures. Indeed, when the coefficient of variation is 50 per cent, there are only two providers publishing prices for those day-case procedures.

Table 7.1: Procedure prices 1994/95 – West Midlands acute hospitals

Procedure[1]	Price per consultant episode			Range	CV	Providers
In-patient	*Ave. £*	*High £*	*Low £*	*£*	*%*	*No.*
Total colectomy	2,773	3,616	558	3,058	21	22
Varicose veins	534	878	334	544	26	24
Ingrowing toenail	347	691	233	458	24	18
Skin biopsy	457	801	275	526	24	18
Lymph node excision	568	1,062	317	745	23	22
Day-case						
Total colectomy	390	600	179	421	50	2
Varicose veins	322	519	179	340	29	24
Ingrowing toenail	237	485	69	416	19	27
Skin biopsy	224	485	69	416	18	27
Lymph node excision	290	539	169	370	27	25

1 The above general surgery procedure prices were selected from 113 published procedure prices within the specialties of ophthalmology, ENT, general surgery, urology, gynaecology and orthopaedics.

However, several DMUs/trusts are charging the same price for all *day-case* procedures within a specialty. Indeed, one DMU did not differentiate between specialty *in-patient* procedures for GPFHs, though admittedly the DMU only provided a small number of procedures. There must surely be differing resource use between procedures, not least because of the differing length of stay associated with individual in-patient procedures. On examining the day-case prices, it was found that the price variations were often largely explained by the crude pricing structure. For example, one DMU used one price for all general surgery procedures; this provider had the lowest price for 20 out of the 35 GPFH general surgery procedures. One trust banded the procedures into just three bands;

this trust had the highest price for 15 out of the 35 GPFH general surgery procedures. Although generally variations in prices between providers had reduced from the 1991 survey position, wide variations in prices still occurred. The price for the treatment of an ingrowing toenail varied from £69 to £691: from £233 to £691 for in-patient treatment and from £69 to £485 for day-case treatment. Did these prices indicate comparative efficiency? It was apparent that a significant amount of the variation related to the crude and inconsistent pricing structure adopted by some providers. Did the remainder relate to comparative efficiency? Had cost accounting methods for pricing healthcare developed to overcome the deficiencies detailed in the previous chapter? This is considered through the questionnaire survey.

7.4 The 1994 questionnaire survey

The 1994 questionnaire was supported by the West Midlands Research Group of the HFMA (Healthcare Financial Managers Association) who provided the contact points at the acute service providers (25 DMUs and trusts) in the West Midlands Health Region (Table 7.2). There had been many mergers of healthcare providers in the previous three years, and NHS trusts/ DMUs were now larger than in 1991. Sixteen questionnaires were returned (64 per cent response rate).

The fifteen DMUs and trusts which reported their contract income had combined contract income of over £814m. Individual DMU/ trust income varied from as little as £9m to over £148m (Figure 7.1a). There was a marked change in the size of provider organisations in 1994 compared with 1991. In 1991, 27 per cent of providers had budgets below £10m; by 1994 only one of the sixteen providers responding to the questionnaire had a budget below £10m. In 1991 only three out of 36 providers had budgets above £50m; in the 1994 survey, seven out of fifteen had budgets above £50m (Figure 7.1b). Correspondingly, small providers with budgets below £10m accounted for 6 per cent of expenditure in the 1991 survey and only 1 per cent in 1994 (Figure 7.1c).

Table 7.2: Acute service providers in the West Midlands Region 1994

District Health Authority	DMU/ Trust
North Worcestershire	Alexandra Healthcare NHST
	Kidderminster Healthcare NHST
Herefordshire	Hereford Hospitals NHST
Worcester and District	Worcester Royal Infirmary NHST
Shropshire	Royal Shrewsbury Hospital NHST
	Princess Royal Hospital NHST
	Robert Jones & Agnes Hunt NHST
North Staffordshire	North Staffordshire Hospitals NHST
South Staffordshire	Burton Hospitals NHST
	Mid Staffordshire General Hospitals NHST
	Rugby NHST
Warwickshire	George Eliot Hospital NHST
	South Warwickshire Hospitals NHST
South Birmingham	South Birmingham Acute Unit
	Birmingham Children's Hospital
North Birmingham	Birmingham Heartlands Hospital NHST
	Good Hope Hospital
	Dudley Road – City Hospital
	Single Specialty Acute Services
Coventry	Walsgrave Hospitals NHST
Dudley	Dudley Group of Hospitals NHST
Sandwell	Sandwell Healthcare NHST
Solihull	Solihull Hospital
Walsall	Walsall Hospitals NHST
Wolverhampton	Royal Wolverhampton NHST

Figure 7.1a: Expenditure of DMUs/trusts in the 1994 survey

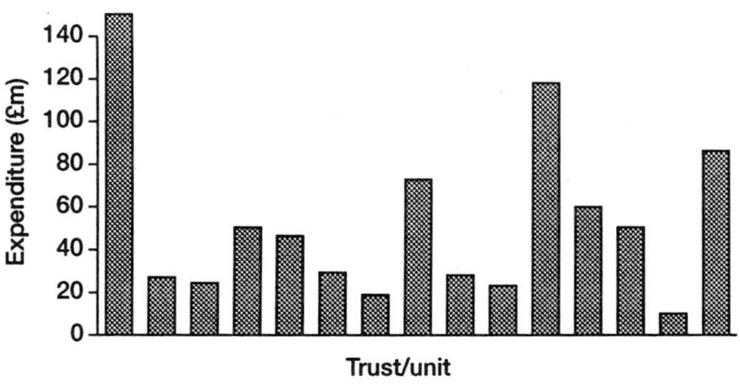

Figure 7.1b: DMUs/trusts in the 1994 survey analysed by size £

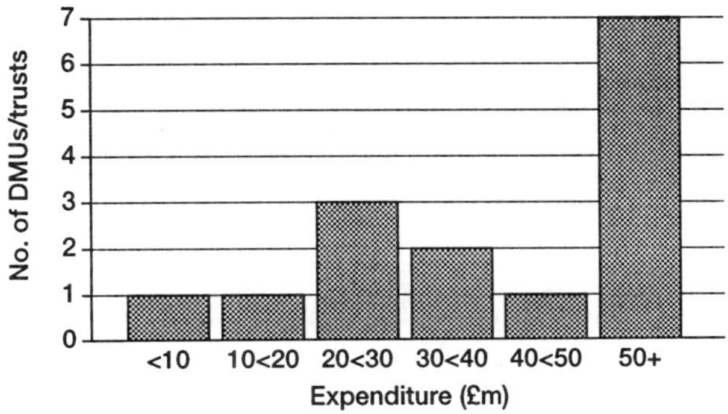

Figure 7.1c: Total service expenditure by DMU/trust size

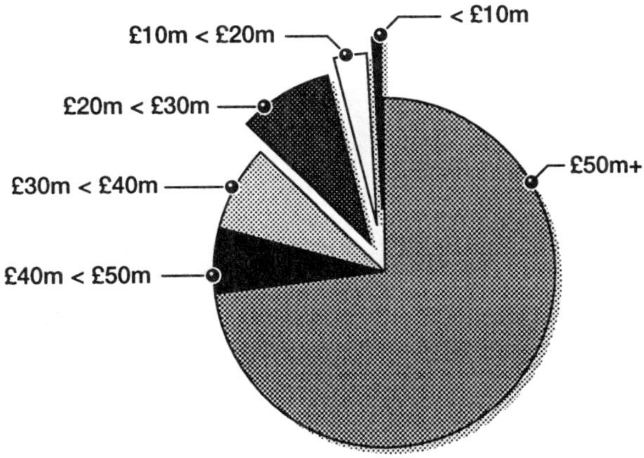

7.5 *Market changes*

Some movement towards contracts related more closely to activity (i.e. from block contracts to cost and volume or cost per case) was evident (Table 7.3).

Relating prices to activity is seen as fundamental in using market mechanisms to encourage economic efficiency; without it, purchasers cannot make rational choices between providers, and providers will still be impeded in their attempts to become more efficient because of the 'efficiency trap'.

Table 7.3: The form of contracts placed 1994/95

Type of contract	% of contract income	
	1991/92	1994/95
Block	28	26
Block with indicative volume	61	58
Cost and volume	8	11
Cost per case	3	5
Total	100	100

The number of providers and HA purchasers is decreasing. In 1991/92 a provider contracted on average with ten HAs and two GPFHs. By 1994/95 many providers had merged (as had four purchasing authorities), but a provider on average contracted with nine HAs and seven GPFHs. Thus in 1994 the market in the West Midlands consisted of fewer but bigger providers and purchasers; the market was becoming more oligopolistic. Although many market proponents (e.g. *Baumol et al.*, 1988) would argue that it is the threat of potential competition, rather than competition *per se,* that is important, the dangers of monopolistic behaviour would seem to be increasing and ensuring contestability must be increasingly difficult (because of the heavy investment and specialist resources required) as the market becomes more concentrated.

7.6 *Development of the cost methods behind the prices*

In the survey, over half of the provider units/trusts regarded the 1993 NHSME guidance as requiring substantial or major revision to their cost attribution process (Table 7.4).

The main areas of revision identified were:

- the additional cost classification and analysis (i.e. variable, semi-fixed and fixed; and direct, indirect and overhead);
- the two-stage apportionment of indirect/overhead costs;
- the apportionment bases.

Table 7.4: Revision to the cost attribution process, 1994/95 contracts

Revision	No. of providers	Percentage
Major	2	13
Substantial	8	50
Minor	5	31
No revision	1	6
Total	16	100

Cost classification and analysis

Cost classification

Prior to the 1994/95 costing and pricing round, only two providers identified cost behaviour using variable, semi-fixed and fixed classifications; a further two providers used variable and fixed classifications. If providers in the NHS internal market are to be able to price contracts on a cost basis confidently for varying levels of activity, it is important to be able to assess cost–volume changes with reasonable precision. The NHS *Costing for Contracting Manual* provides brief definitions of the classifications:

> *Fixed costs*
>
> *'Costs should be regarded as fixed costs if they are unaffected by in-year activity changes in a one-year period.'*
>
> *Semi-fixed costs*
>
> *'Semi-fixed costs, otherwise known as step costs, are those that are fixed for a given range of activity, but may increase or fall as activity rises to, or drops below, specific levels of activity, i.e. they are partly affected by changes in activity.'*
>
> *Variable costs*
>
> *'Variable costs are those that tend to vary with the level of activity, and in such a way that a near proportionate change in cost accompanies a change in activity.'* *NHSME* (1993c)

In the 1994 survey, 75 per cent of providers expressed no difficulty in undertaking the required analysis. The remaining 25 per cent identified the following problems:

- current budget analysis does not allow easy identification of variable costs;
- difficulty in establishing timescale 'so many fell into semi-fixed' ;
- some classifications need refining;
- disagree with some classifications, e.g. treatment of computer hardware as semi-fixed.

The above comments are likely to express problems encountered by many healthcare providers. The 1991 survey showed the use of budget data for contract price determination rather than historical cost; by 1994 this had become the norm. However, the NHSME guidance for cost classification is based on the annual reporting categories. The use of these categories by the NHSME is understandable as they had been previously prescribed for use throughout the health service for many years, but it is inevitable that they will not correlate easily with the budget categories designed and used for internal management purposes.

The second comment (so many costs falling into the semi-fixed category) is also a major difficulty with the cost classification in terms of its usefulness to aid the contracting process. The bulk of hospital expenditure falls into this category. For example, nursing costs alone account for roughly 50 per cent of hospital expenditure. There is no doubt that if activity increases sufficiently more nurses are required and vice versa, but it is the understanding of the 'step' that is important to the contracting process; without such knowledge the classifications have very limited use.

As the third comment implies, the classifications are set at such a broad level, it is inevitable that they cannot be realistically applied without refinement. Indeed, the *Manual* actually states that where providers are able, they should analyse costs at a lower level to improve the level of classification and analysis achieved. Consequently there is considerable scope for inconsistency.

The ranges for the total level of variable, semi-fixed and fixed costs at each provider unit or trust are shown in Table 7.5.

Table 7.5: Cost classification, 1994/95 contracts

Cost classification	Range as % of total cost	Average
Variable	1.2 to 26	12
Semi-fixed	50 to 88.8	64
Fixed	10 to 31.5	22

Vast variations in analysed cost behaviour are apparent, casting doubt on whether all providers used a similar approach to the analysis (Figure 7.2). If the provider with the extremely low level of variable costs is removed the ranges are 7 to 26 per cent for variable costs, 50 to 68 per cent for semi-fixed and 11 to 31.5 per cent for fixed costs (these ranges are apparently wider than those found by the NHSME reference sites (*NHSME*, 1993c, Figure 7.B.1). Variations by specialty were great. The specialties identified as having relatively high levels of variable costs are: anaesthetics (up to 64 per cent), oncology (up to 36 per cent) and haematology (up to 44 per cent). Low variable cost specialties are obstetrics, paediatrics and geriatric medicine.

Figure 7.2: Cost classification – survey DMUs/trusts 1994

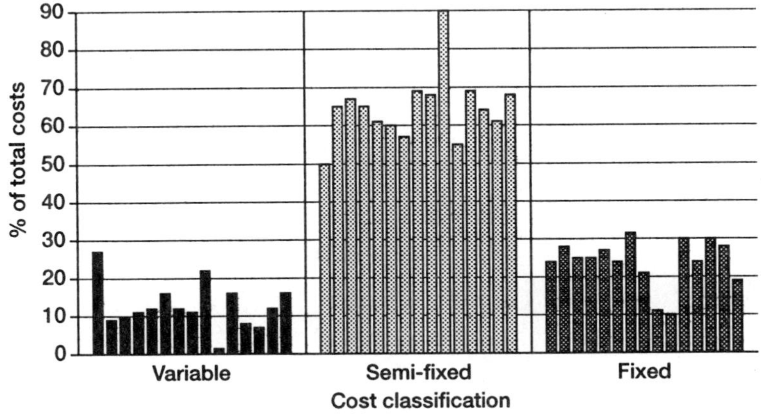

Cost analysis by type

Only two provider units/ trusts expressed any difficulty in analysing costs as direct, indirect or overhead. Expressed difficulties related to multi-specialty wards and direct *department* costs as opposed to *specialty*. The current guidance does little to remedy these problems:

> *'The analysis of costs as direct, indirect and overheads should be in relation to specialty ... wherever possible. Otherwise it should be in relation to wards/departments/cost centres.'*
>
> *NHSME* (1993d)

The classification of costs as direct, etc., depends on the cost object. At present NHS costing is still grappling with the problem of identifying appropriate 'products' for costing and pricing purposes, therefore the guidance cannot be precise on this issue.

The ranges for the total level of direct, indirect and overhead costs at each provider unit or trust are as shown in Table 7.6. Only ten DMUs/trusts provided the analysis; two stated that they were unable to provide such analysis at that time.

Table 7.6: Direct, indirect and overhead costs, 1994/95 contracts

Cost analysis	Range: % of total £	Average
Direct	20 to 60	45
Indirect	11 to 49	28
Overhead	19 to 42	27

The variation in the analysis of total provider costs into direct, indirect and overhead categories by individual DMUs/trusts is shown in Figure 7.3.

Figure 7.3: Cost analysis – survey DMUs/trusts 1994

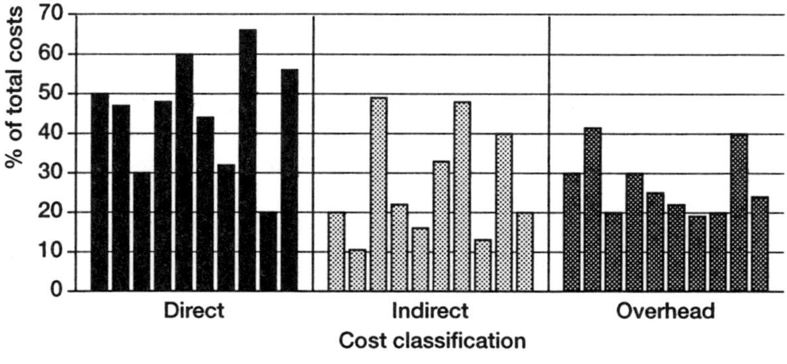

The range of direct costs within specialties at individual provider units and trusts is much greater. For example, at one provider unit/trust, the level of direct costs varies according to specialty from 4 per cent to 74 per cent, while a further provider unit/trust has a variation from 8 per cent to 82 per cent. Obstetrics was most frequently stated as the specialty with the highest level of direct costs.

Fifty per cent of the provider units and trusts did not convert the local budget costs into nationally recognised categories prior to cost classification and analysis. This may partly be because the requirement was not made explicit in the earlier guidance and the *Manual* was not received until September 1993 after the costing for pricing process was well under way in most units and trusts. The *Costing for Contracting Manual* states:

> *'To enable national guidance on allocation and apportionment methods to be applied to local management and budget structures, it is necessary to regroup or convert the local budget costs into nationally recognised categories, i.e.: 'TFR1/ HFR21 Hospital and Community Services – Departmental Analysis'. This enables the allocation and apportionment methods ... to be applied to each department in a standardised way that can be replicated.'* *NHSME* (1993c)

Some providers stated that there was 'no reason to do so' or 'no need', while most nonconformists pointed out that their own budgets were at a more detailed level and therefore enabled more detailed cost apportionments to be applied than could be achieved through TFR1/ HFR21 groupings.

Two-stage apportionment of indirect/overhead costs

A staged (step-down) approach

The guidance puts forward a two-stage process for the attribution of indirect or overhead costs to specialties:

> *'a two-stage apportionment of support services, via patient treatment services, to specialty is recommended where appropriate. In this way patient treatment services which require relatively high levels of support services will channel their costs through to the specialties they serve.'* *NHSME* (1993c)

This recommendation develops costing for contracting along the lines set out in section 4.5. Direct apportionment of non-patient treatment departments to patient treatment services is acceptable under NHSME guidance, but more sophisticated approaches are not precluded. One provider, however, used a 10 per cent uplift to specialty costs to cover general overhead items, and a further two providers attributed all support services directly to specialties rather than via patient treatment services. Considerable variation was apparent as regards which support services were attributed using a staged approach (Table 7.7).

Table 7.7: Support services attributed via patient treatment services (PTS)

Support service	% of providers attributing via PTS
Domestic	81
Catering	62
Laundry	69
Portering/transport	87
Building/engineering maintenance	81
Site overheads	69
General management	75

Table 7.7 shows an improvement in both the level of sophistication in costing and consistency between providers. For example, the 1991 survey found only 50 per cent of providers attributing domestic services to PTS, 28 per cent of portering/transport and 28 per cent of building or engineering maintenance. However, a significant level of overhead and indirect costs continue to be apportioned directly to specialties.

The apportionment bases

Twenty per cent of provider units and trusts used less than the minimum standard apportionment base specified in the *Costing for Contracting Manual.* The main areas where other apportionment bases were substituted were building and engineering maintenance, energy, training and education, pathology, laundry/linen, porters/transport and theatres. One provider stated that theatre sessions were used rather than minutes partly because the minutes data was suspect, but also because sessions were regarded as a better determinant of cost.

Cost/resource management systems

Two-thirds of the provider units and trusts reported incurring no additional costs for the 1994/95 costing and pricing exercise. The highest reported additional cost was £22,500. The most commonly used computer software in the West Midlands Region for costing for contracting is the Specialty and Procedure Pricing System (SAPPS) which is used by half of the provider units and trusts in the survey; 38 per cent of providers use in-house systems often based on Lotus spreadsheets. Two providers linked their spreadsheets to their case-mix or HISS system. Three systems in particular (The Accountant – SECTA, Thorn EMI DRG Cost Model and the Bradford–Calderdale) were not used by any of the respondents to the survey for the 1994/95 costing and pricing exercise; all three systems were identified as commonly used systems by the NHSME EL(93)26.

However, the future development of the costing for pricing systems to treatment categories, as indicated by the NHSME in FDL(93)51 and later included as Chapter 3 in the *Costing for Contracting Manual*, requires heavy investment in activity information systems owing to the current lack of resource management information. Case-mix management systems were only operational at a third of the provider units and trusts. With the exception of pharmacy, computerised activity information was not normally available for many patient treatment services, as shown in Table 7.8.

Table 7.8: Operational activity information systems

Computer system	% of providers 1991/92	1994/95
Case mix	0	38
Nursing dependency	15	25
Pharmacy	44	88
Theatre	15	38
Pathology	36	50
Radiology	23	25

Case-mix databases are very expensive to install and operate. Brunel University estimated that the six pilot resource management hospitals made over £1m investment each in information systems alone with no measurable improvements in patient care (*Packwood et al.*, 1991).

Two-thirds of providers felt that their existing cost and information systems were inadequate for meeting the further NHSME guidance on costing for pricing contracts below specialty level.

Pricing below specialty level

Providers must price below specialty level for GPFH procedures. GPFH procedures relate mainly to elective surgery; these are a subset of OPCS4 procedure codes and thus more numerous and specific than HRGs. In 1994 the cost information for GPFH prices was often based on estimated resource usage rather than determined through a systematic costing exercise which analyses total costs for each cost component. Nevertheless, GPFH pricing has become more sophisticated (Table 7.9).

Table 7.9: The cost components of GPFH procedure prices

Cost component	% of providers	
	1991/92	1994/95
Average specialty cost per day	100	100
Theatre costs	49	62
Drugs	15	25
Prostheses	54	88

Although 56 per cent of provider units and trusts charge some purchasers, other than GPFHs, prices calculated at below specialty level there is little consistency in the sub-specialty groupings used. Sometimes providers use their own classifications to band treatments into routine/complex or major/intermediate/minor; some providers choose to price a few significant procedures separately. Two providers used the GPFH procedure prices for all purchasers. Where this is not followed, some cross-subsidisation between purchasers is inevitable.

The effect on purchaser contract prices

The survey was undertaken in January 1994, at the commencement of the contract negotiations for 1994/95 contracts. It was therefore too early to establish the extent to which the cost analysis and classification was made available to purchasers. Such openness was clearly encouraged in the NHSME guidance, but the NHSME stopped short of making disclosure obligatory. Only one provider had distributed information on cost behaviour to purchasers for 1993/94 contract negotiations, but providers may have made other cost information available to purchasers, especially host purchasers.

The provider units and trusts were asked to identify the number of their purchasers whose contract quantum had changed significantly because of changes to the method of costing and pricing contracts. However, no providers identified cost shifts per purchaser over £500,000 resulting from their revised costing and pricing system. Only two providers identified cost shifts affecting individual purchaser(s) by more than £100,000. Neither of these providers was particularly large – they had quantum of cost at or below £50m and several DHA purchasers (the survey covered provider units and trusts with quantum of costs ranging from £9m to £148m). Given the substantial or major revision to the costing system reported by the majority of providers, it is surprising that cost shifts were not more prevalent. It may be that cost shifts between specialties may not have resulted in large shifts in individual HA contracts because of the mix of specialties purchased by HAs. On the other hand, the case studies show that the effects of the cost changes were sometimes manipulated (Chapters 9 and 10 below). As reported at the start of this section, the number of providers and HA purchasers is decreasing. The market is dominated by a few (usually) knowledgeable negotiators who agree contracts covering many products including non-price aspects of service delivery. In such circumstances, neo-classical economic theory propounds that it is highly unlikely that cost will be the major determinant of price. If the neo-Austrian perspective is taken, then while oligopoly or even monopoly is not necessarily detrimental to efficiency, pricing will be a matter of strategy; only if the market is clearly contestable can the providers be expected to strive to be efficient.

7.7 *Survey findings and implications*

- Price comparisons for DHA contracts and ECRs were difficult because of the lack of consistent contract categories.
- Price variations for GPFH procedures were partly due to the crude pricing structures used by some providers.
- The costing for contracting guidance has required most providers (63 per cent) to substantially revise their approach to costing and pricing contracts.
- Seventy-five per cent of providers expressed no difficulty in applying

the guidance regarding the additional cost classification (fixed; semi-fixed; variable). However, the considerable variation reported regarding the level of such costs casts doubt on whether the guidance is consistently applied.

- Similarly, the vast majority of providers reported no problems concerning the cost analysis by type, but large variations are apparent between individual providers.
- Half the providers did not regroup their budgets into nationally recognised categories in order to consistently apply the guidance.
- Only one provider reported using a percentage uplift to cover general overhead items. The majority of providers are adopting a two-staged approach to attribute support services, but there are instances of providers placing all their support service costs direct to specialties rather than passing them through patient treatment services.
- Minimum standard apportionment bases were generally achieved.
- SAPPS and in-house spreadsheet systems are widely used by providers in the West Midlands.
- Only one-third of providers reported incurring additional costs on their costing for pricing exercise for 1994/95 contracts. The highest reported cost was £22,500.
- Case-mix and other resource management systems are not available in most provider units and trusts.
- Considerable development is necessary to achieve systematic costing and pricing using consistent contract categories below specialty level.
- Some progress towards contracts related more closely to activity was apparent, but block contracts still predominate.
- Surprisingly few cost shifts between purchasers were reported.

The guidance sought to achieve consistency and a minimum level of sophistication in costing for contracting. The West Midlands survey shows that consistency has improved, but it is far from assured. Greater clarity, timeliness and compulsion is necessary if increased consistency is required. Although the guidance for the 1994/95 contracts has been implemented fairly cheaply and easily (albeit to varying degrees), the development of costing for contracting below specialty level is likely to be much more onerous.

On completion of the 1991 survey it was expected that progress in costing for contracting would be as set out in Figure 6.3, the internal market continuum; the deficiencies of NHS cost information were evident, but there was a clear perception of where the market was leading. However, progress along the internal market continuum has been slow: only a small shift away from block contracts had materialised by 1994. Standard contract categories based on procedures had not been implemented, although the intention that they be used to inform the contracting process in some specialties for 1995/96 had been established. The move towards procedure costing will increase the very limited use of 'bottom-up' costing, and there was evidence in 1994 of an increase in departmental cost/activity systems. However, there was still a dearth of information and resources required for more accurate cost attribution, especially at procedure level.

More fundamentally, the survey has queried whether the approach to contract pricing needs to be reassessed in the light of the developing market. The 1993 NHSME guidance sought to facilitate the market's efficiency aims by endeavouring to make prices reliable indicators of relative efficiency and therefore feed appropriate signals to the market to enable an improved distribution of NHS resources. However, there are indications that comparability and consistency will be extremely difficult to ensure, particularly as the market environment may not be conducive to a uniform, full-cost-based pricing mechanism.

7.8 Summary

This chapter has examined how cost-based pricing has developed after three years of the NHS internal market and after detailed guidance had been issued by the NHSME. The conditions necessary for price signals to encourage economic efficiency were still not apparent. Some progress towards contracts more closely related to activity had been made, but the vast bulk of provider income still came from block contracts. Inadequate product definition, and indeed the lack of even uniform specialty pricing, made efficiency comparisons between providers for much of their workload impossible. Where products were more clearly and consistently defined (e.g. GPFH procedures) some of the price variation was due to the crude pricing methods used. The cost methods behind the prices had improved and the NHSME guidance had led to increased consistency, but there were examples of non-compliance and there was much local subjectivity surrounding application of the guidance. There was still a lack of activity systems to enable even direct patient care costs to be attributed accurately to specialties and most importantly to enable more meaningful, consistent contract categories to be used below specialty level. The costing for contracting process and the issues surrounding it are examined in more depth in the case studies in the following two chapters.

8
The Case Studies – Costing for Pricing

8.1 Introduction

The preceding two chapters have provided an overview of cost-based pricing in the first year of the market and three years into the market. A more detailed picture of the costing and pricing process is developed through the use of case studies. This chapter provides an in-depth view of the costing for pricing process. Firstly, the two acute healthcare providers used as case studies are set out; the 1993/94 costing for contracting approach and the resultant prices are examined before studying the 1994/95 contracting round. The cost model adopted by each case is set out and the thinking behind it; the perception and effect of the NHSME guidance on the costing process is examined and the approach to costing product lines investigated.

8.2 The two acute healthcare providers

Two case studies with different geographic environments, size and complexity of service provision were chosen.

The St Somewhere Trust

St Somewhere NHST has a budget of £90 million and more than 4000 staff. The trust comprises two hospital sites in a large conurbation; it has over 1200 beds with supporting out-patient departments. The hospitals are resource management/hospital information support system pilot sites, the first phase of which has been implemented. The largest hospital had become an NHS trust on 1 April 1992, but it had merged with a neighbouring directly managed hospital on 1 April 1993 to form a new, larger trust.

The trust has a management structure consisting of ten clinical directorates:

Support directorates	Specialty-based directorates
Pathology	Women and children's
Radiology	Orthopaedic
Theatres	Cardiac
Therapy	Surgery
	Medicine
	Radiotherapy

Each clinical director is supported by a business manager and a senior nurse where appropriate. The income of St Somewhere in 1993/94 is set out in Table 8.1.

Table 8.1: 1993/94 income of St Somewhere Trust

Purchaser	% of contract and ECR income 1993/94
DHAs in the West Midlands:	
1	70
2	5
3	2
4	–
5	–
Regional Specialties	19
Sub-total (West Midlands)	96
DHA outside West Midlands	1
GPFHs	1
ECRs	1
Total	100

Source: *St Somewhere Corporate Contract 1993/94*

In 1993/94, the trust received 70 per cent of its contract income from its host DHA and a further 19 per cent from regional speciality work (which is devolved from the RHA to the DHAs for 1994/95 contracts). The GPFH income was less than 2 per cent of contract income, but was set to double when new fundholders joined the scheme in 1994/95. The trust, despite being in a large conurbation, had not had a high level of income at risk in the early years of the market, but the level of income at risk is increasing sharply.

Thereabouts acute unit

The Thereabouts Unit was directly managed by its host purchasing authority in 1993/94, but became a trust on 1 April 1994. Thereabouts Unit comprises three hospitals in a small city of a shire county. The hospitals have a budget of £30 million, provide 455 in-patient beds and employ over 1700 people.

Thereabouts Unit has four clinical directorates: support services (including pathology and radiology); surgery; medicine; and women and children's services. Each directorate has a clinical director and a business manager. The unit's contract income is analysed in Table 8.2.

Table 8.2: 1993/94 income of Thereabouts Unit

Purchaser	% of contract and ECR income 1993/94
DHAs in the West Midlands	
1	76
2	2
3	–
4	–
Sub-total (West Midlands)	78
DHAs outside West Midlands	10
GPFHs	11
ECRs	1
Total	100

Source: *Thereabouts Unit Corporate Contract 1993/94*

In 1993/94, 76 per cent of the Thereabouts Unit's contract and ECR income came from the host DHA. Despite being located in a rural area, the unit has a significant amount of risk income; in 1993/94 11 per cent of its income was from GPFHs, and this was to increase to over 12 per cent in 1994/95.

8.3 The costing processes for 1993/94 contracts

The costing processes for 1993/94 of the two case studies varied markedly. The main aspects are summarised in Table 8.3. These costing approaches were adopted before the NHSME issued the detailed guidance which later formed the NHS *Costing for Contracting Manual* (see section 6.2).

Table 8.3: Costing approaches 1993/94 contract pricing

	St Somewhere Trust	Thereabouts Unit
Cost attribution	All purchasers – GPFH procedures priced separately with remainder of work at average specialty price	Two-stage approach for • capital charges • estates • general overhead No % uplift to specialty costs for remote overheads, but many support service costs apportioned direct to specialties.
Cost analysis	Locally determined: • fixed • semi-fixed • variable	None undertaken
Cost type	Capital charges Revenue expenditure	Capital charges Revenue expenditure
Contract categories	DHAs – specialties GPFHs – procedures ECRs – banded procedures (major, intermediate and minor)	All purchasers: GPFH procedures priced separately with remainder of work at average specialty price

Cost attribution

The St Somewhere Trust used a framework of cost flows whereby capital charges and four categories of overhead (telecommunications, estate, finance and domestic services) were attributed using a staged (step-down) approach as described in section 4.4. Fifty-eight per cent of budget costs were attributed direct to specialties. Seven per cent of budget costs were treated as a general overhead and added as a percentage uplift to the specialty costs (after inclusion of other overhead and indirect items).

The Thereabouts Unit used a framework of cost flows which attributed all general overheads through service departments except for personnel and telephone costs, which were added as a percentage uplift to gross specialty costs. However, a further 10 per cent in the form of support service costs were attributed directly to specialties/ contract categories on various apportionment bases (e.g. domestic and portering costs were not fed through patient treatment services).

Neither provider therefore undertook the costing for contracting in the manner later set out by the NHSME guidance: St Somewhere and Thereabouts did not build up the full cost of patient treatment service departments. St Somewhere only attributed four categories of overhead, whereas Thereabouts attributed most overheads but often attributed support service costs directly to specialties. Obviously, different methods of cost attribution will affect the prices derived.

Cost analysis

The St Somewhere Trust had developed a system of cost analysis in recent years: costs were analysed as fixed, semi-variable and variable. The analysis was based on local understanding of cost behaviour: 12 per cent of hospital expenditure was classified as variable, 51 per cent semi-variable and 37 per cent as fixed. Most non-staff costs were included as variable, with the exception of maintenance contracts which were regarded as fixed; staff costs were regarded as semi-variable or fixed. The Thereabouts Unit did not include any analysis of costs by behaviour.

Cost type

Costs were classified at both providers according to whether they related to capital charges (depreciation and interest) or revenue expenditure. The costs were not classified as overhead, indirect and direct as later stipulated in the NHSME guidance.

Contract categories

The St Somewhere Trust compiled costs by specialty. These were used for specialty prices for DHA purchasers and adapted using information from an earlier bottom-up costing exercise for GPFH procedures. ECRs were priced by classifying procedures into bands, i.e. major, intermediate and minor (based on BUPA groupings).

The Thereabouts Unit compiled costs by specialty. These were used to compile GPFH procedure prices using specialty in-patient day with some bottom-up costing for theatre costs and prostheses. The GPFH procedure prices were used for all purchasers. Thus a tonsillectomy would be charged at the same price under a DHA contract, a GPFH contract or as an ECR. A DHA contract would also include work priced at average specialty cost for the remaining (i.e. non-GPFH) procedures.

Costing software

At St Somewhere the prices were derived using a software package SAPPS (Speciality and Procedure Pricing System) into which nearly 3000 budget lines were entered. This system is used by over 100 units and trusts (*NHSME*, 1993a). The system uses a relational database for calculating costs by the 'top-down' approach. The Thereabouts Unit derived costs and prices from the unit's budget summaries using Lotus spreadsheets.

1993/94 prices

The resultant prices differed markedly between the two providers. A dermatology in-patient stay is £1998 at the trust compared with £2823 at the unit, but an in-patient stay in paediatric medicine is £988 at the trust compared with £496 at the unit. The two providers were often difficult to compare as they identified treatments in different ways. Two examples are given below:

- The trust priced a general medicine in-patient at £1051 on its ECR price list. The unit charged £776 but this excluded the intensive therapy unit (ITU) or the coronary care unit (CCU). Not all general medicine cases would require a stay in ITU and/or CCU and therefore it is impossible to compare prices specifically.

- The trust priced a tonsillectomy on its GPFH price list as £686 for an in-patient stay and £154 for a day case, but on its ECR tariffs a tonsillectomy was priced at £568; for the unit, the charge was £646 (in-patient only) for all purchasers. The differing prices charged for tonsillectomy at St Somewhere obviously relate to the differing approaches adopted for costing each form of contract or ECR tariff. A patient would receive the same treatment whether referred under a DHA contract, by a GPFH or as an ECR; apart from the separation of in-patient and day-case treatment the variations provide no indication of relative efficiency.

The two providers are unlikely to be in direct competition because of their locations. However, it would appear that purchasers in the market could have considerable difficulty in ensuring that they were comparing like with like even before quality and outcome factors are considered.

8.4 The costing processes for 1994/95 contracts

In early summer 1993 both providers reviewed their approach to costing for contracting in the light of the NHSME guidance. Despite the obvious differences in approach, both providers felt that they were already in line with the overall thrust of the guidance in terms of cost attribution: they had used a staged approach for some overhead/ support costs and had used apportionment bases at or above the specified minimum. Both providers had used numerous apportionment bases for attributing indirect and overhead budgets. The variations from the guidance were considered minor (e.g. using building area rather than volume for attributing estate utility costs, and attributing employee service costs through a percentage uplift rather than apportioning on staff numbers). However, in the 1994 questionnaire, both St Somewhere Trust and Thereabouts Unit regarded the revision of the costing approach to be substantial.

The Director of Finance and Contracting at St Somewhere regarded 'ownership' of the costing data and resultant prices as being of prime importance. He wished to be able to produce 'trading accounts' for each directorate. This required the assignment of contract income to directorates and the assignment of costs according to their recovery through contracts. This requirement, together with the NHSME requirements, led to the following coding matrix being prescribed to link cost analysis with budgetary control.

Figure 8.1: Cost analysis and control: Coding matrix – St Somewhere Trust

	Managed and recovered in directorate's prices			Managed, not recovered in directorate's prices			Not managed, recovered directorate's prices		
	Direct	Indirect	O'head	Direct	Indirect	O'head	Direct	Indirect	O'head
Fixed Semi-fixed Variable									

The St Somewhere Trust embarked on a five-stage approach to costing for 1994/95 contracts using the SAPP system (Figure 8.2).

The new approach was influenced partly by the guidance which required a two-stage approach feeding all costs through patient treatment departments as a minimum. However, a major influence on the approach was the need to improve 'ownership' of the pricing data at (clinical) directorate level and to enable contract income to be compared with budgets at directorate level. The result was a move towards the NHSME uniform approach, for example, reducing the overheads not fed through patient treatment services to a very small percentage. On the other hand, the new approach did not ensure that the full costs of theatres and other treatment areas were available to facilitate development of costing on contract categories below specialty. This was not seen as necessary: 'we do not price at that level'. The new approach was very cumbersome and detailed, with little relation to the 57 uniform expenditure heads set out in the *Costing Manual*.

The Financial Controller at the Thereabouts Unit prepared two papers for business managers and clinical directors in July 1993: one making price comparisons of 1993/94 prices with neighbouring provider units and one proposing a costing for pricing strategy for 1994/95. The former paper concluded that Thereabouts Unit was competitive on average specialty prices but above average for GPFH procedures. The second paper proposed establishing prices in the same manner as previously (i.e. same product lines), but to include the additional analysis and classification set out by the NHSME. After discussion with senior managers, this strategy was adopted subject to:

Figure 8.2 The costing for pricing model – St Somewhere's Trust

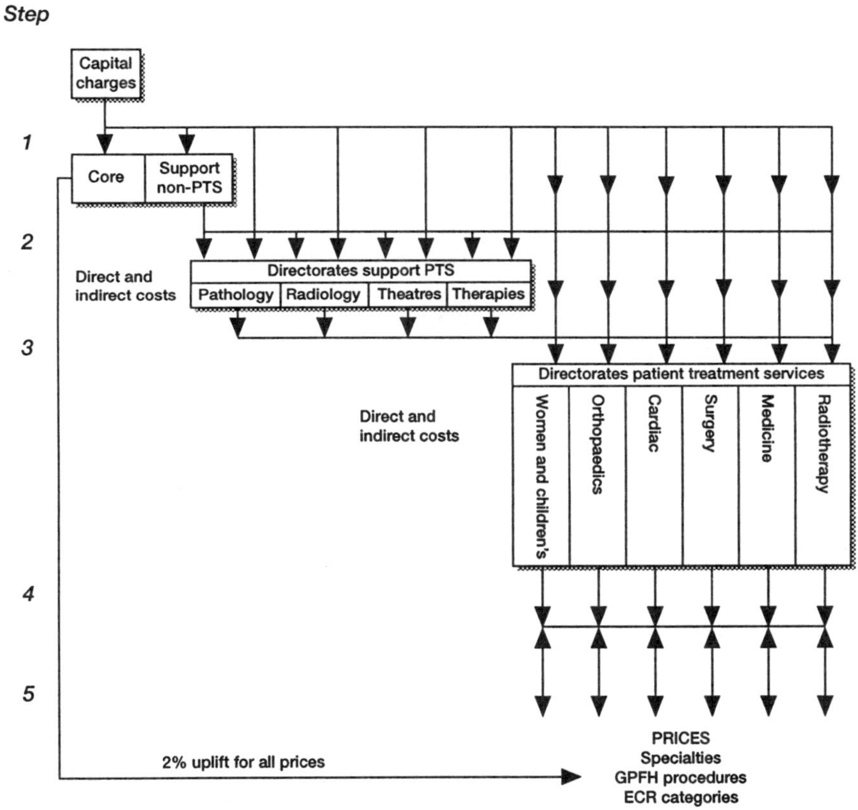

STEPS

1 Capital charges allocated and apportioned to departments

2 Non-treatment departments apportioned to clinical directorates

3 Support directorates apportioned to user directorates and direct access

4 User directorates cross-charge for services between directorates

5 User directorates assigned to contract categories and uplift for core services

'The need to possibly correct any GPFH procedure prices which are at variance with the average.
The possibility of charging a higher rate for emergency cases.'
(Senior Managers Meeting, 18 August 1993)

The Thereabouts Unit had recently introduced the KPMG case-mix system and resolved to use the costing module within it (the spreadsheet approach of previous years was regarded as 'too cumbersome to meet the requirements of EL(93)26'). The cost framework would attribute all overhead and indirect costs through patient treatment services except for those where direct to specialties was identified as a suitable method in the *Manual*, e.g. catering. Few modifications to apportionment bases were envisaged. The 1994/95 cost framework is shown in Figure 8.3.

Figure 8.3 The costing for pricing model – Thereabouts Unit

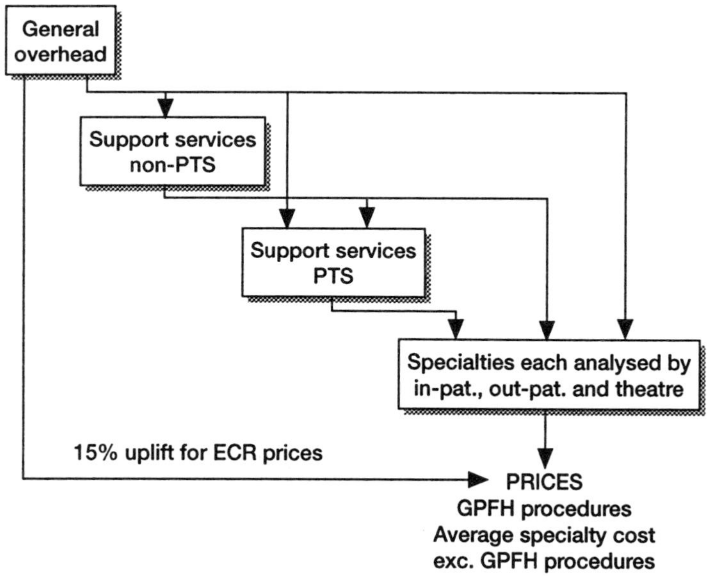

Notes:
General overhead includes administration, finance and insurance
Support services non-PTS includes capital charges, domestics and catering
Support services PTS includes pathology, radiology and therapies

The trust specified budget cost centres and budget lines in the costing system; the unit used cost centres but broke centres down if considered significant for cost attribution. Both providers therefore input cost data in much more detail than broad TFR/FR headings, especially the trust. Neither provider translated their budgets into TFR1/HFR21 nationally recognised categories as required in the Costing Manual. The accountants at both providers had automatically worked from budget lines or summaries as previously, but felt that it would not have materially affected the results anyway. As the accountant at Thereabouts put it:

> *'I would have had to have broken them down again to attribute the costs accurately.'*

Cost analysis and classification

The analysis of costs by type (overhead, indirect and direct) was a new requirement for both providers. The classification of costs into fixed, semi-fixed and variable categories was a further new requirement at the unit. The results are summarised in Table 8.4.

Table 8.4: Cost analysis and classification 1994/95 (case studies)

Case study	*St Somewhere Trust*		*Thereabouts Trust*	
Cost analysis	Average all specialties	Range by specialty[1]	Average all specialties	Range by specialty[2]
Direct	55	93 – 37	50	63 – 44
Indirect	43	63 – 5	20	26 – 11
Overhead	2	Constant	30	35 – 25
Cost classification				
Variable	15	36 – 7	8	9 – 3
Semi-fixed	67	73 – 5	64	75 – 60
Fixed	18	59 – 13	28	31 – 19

1 excluding regional specialties
2 in-patient element only

It is evident that the case study sites have not been consistent in the application of the guidance. The trust used the overhead category to include only very remote overheads added as a percentage uplift to gross specialty costs (i.e. a constant 2 per cent uplift). The Thereabouts Unit applied the guidance rigidly and therefore included maintenance, heating and utilities and administration within this category. The accountant said:

> *'I followed the guidance rigidly, but put no extra thought into it as I do not expect to ever use it! The consultant pathologist went down as per the guidance as "fixed" and "direct".'*

The identification of items as direct, indirect and overhead was difficult because of the ambiguity surrounding what this identification is in relation to; the guidance merely highlights the different interpretations (see section 7.6). Multi-specialty wards were particularly problematic in this respect. Although both case studies had the majority of their costs analysed as direct, this does not mean that they were direct costs of the specialties. Many were direct costs of individual departments (e.g. pathology), but these costs were then apportioned to specialties. A number of grey areas were found in addition to multi-specialty wards, but were not subject to rigorous consideration because of the little value placed on the information.

The budget data did not always lend itself to the current subjective analysis headings (from the annual accounts) used in the guidance. The later version of the guidance included in the *Costing Manual* adds that the classification and cost analysis given

> *'oversimplifies the classification in some areas. Where providers are able, they should analyse costs at a lower level to improve the classification/ analysis achieved.'* *NHSME* (1993c)

The accountants at both providers saw little value in the classification/analysis, although both undertook the work from a lower level because of the budget input used. At the trust, the classification of costs into fixed, semi-fixed and variable was often influenced by their earlier approach. For example, maintenance contracts continued to be classed as 'fixed' despite the guidance stipulating semi-fixed. Most of the other non-staff expenditure was regarded as variable. The accountants at both providers would not use the analysis for any decisions: 'at best, it might be a rough starting point'. Thereabouts Unit had a higher proportion of its costs classified as fixed and proportionately more overhead cost; however, this would appear largely due to differing approaches to the classifi-cation and analysis rather than true differences in cost structure.

Apportionment bases

The 1993 guidance stipulated minimum standards for apportionment basis. Both case studies attributed costs in far greater detail than the 57 headings used in the guidance. St Somewhere, initially at least, asked departmental managers to assess how the costs of their department should be attributed to specialties. Thereabouts Unit used apportionment bases similar to those stipulated in the guidance, but frequently more than one apportionment base per department was applied. For example, building and engineering maintenance expenditure was analysed by different classes of staff and then attributed according to time data from planned preventative maintenance schemes, emergency work, etc.

Costing 'product lines' for pricing, 1994/95

St Somewhere Trust compiled cost-based prices in a different manner for each type of purchaser.

DHA purchasers (St Somewhere)

Cost-based prices were compiled using average specialty cost per FCE (finished consultant episode) and per out-patient attendance. These were derived by dividing the specialty costs calculated through the costing model by the expected 1994/95 activity.

GPFHs (St Somewhere)

Procedure prices for GPFHs were largely obtained by deriving the specialty cost per in-patient day and multiplying by the average length of stay for each procedure. Adjustments were made based on earlier costing exercises for theatre time and high-cost items such as prostheses. The costing exercises also formed the basis for day-case procedure prices. However, these adjustments were not systematic as theatres and high-cost items had not been identified separately in the costing model.

ECRs (St Somewhere)

Average specialty cost per FCE was utilised for most specialties, but prices were compiled at a lower level for general surgery, urology, ENT and gynaecology. Within these specialties, high-activity (or possibly high-cost) procedures were priced on the basis of previous costing studies: in ophthalmology the previous bottom-up exercise had covered most ophthalmology procedures; in gynaecology, urology and ENT a small number of procedures were priced separately with the remaining procedures being grouped into bands (minor, intermediate and major); in general surgery all procedures were grouped and two further bands used (major plus and complex). In orthopaedics hip and knee replacements were costed separately, but the remainder were on average specialty. Day cases and out-patients were priced on specialty.

At *Thereabouts Unit*, consistency was maintained between purchasers (apart from the addition of an extra 15 per cent if the work related to an ECR). For each specialty, costs had been attributed to theatres; high-cost items (prostheses, etc.); general (ward costs, etc.); day cases; and out-patients. Prices were then compiled as follows.

For each GPFH procedure (all purchasers)

The cost per specialty in-patient day was multiplied by the ALOS (or if appropriate a day-case rate was used). To this was added the theatre cost (theatre time multiplied by theatre rate) and the cost of any high-cost items.

For example, in ophthalmology, a cataract was priced as follows:

	£
1.9 days @ £193 per day	366.70
55 mins in theatre @ £8.79 per min	483.45
High-cost items	—
Price	850.00

Average specialty price (excluding GPFH procedures)

The balance of specialty costs for in-patient and day-case treatments (i.e. total less cost of GPFH procedures) was divided through by the remaining activity to derive the balance average price for other procedures on an in-patient or day-case basis.

Out-patients

Out-patients were priced separately for each specialty according to whether a procedure is to be undertaken at the attendance, it is a first attendance, or a follow-up attendance. These three types of out-patient attendance were weighted 3:2:1 respectively based on a subjective assessment of the time for each type of assessment. The total specialty cost for out-patients is then divided by the weighted attendances to derive the cost for each type of attendance.

For example, in ophthalmology, the total out-patient cost is £478,748.

Estimated attendances		Weighted attendances
Procedure	347 × 3	1,041
First	1,787 × 2	3,574
Follow-up	11,483 × 1	11,483
Total		16,098

£478,748/16098 = £30

Price per attendance:	
Procedure	£90
First	£60
Follow-up	£30

There was therefore consistency in pricing between purchasers from Thereabouts. The unit generally priced a lower level of service definition than St Somewhere for DHA purchasers. Standard contract categories for at least one specialty (orthopaedics, ophthalmology and gynaecology) were expected to be costed and used by all providers 'to inform contracts for 1995/96' (*NHSME*, 1994a), but it will be much longer before standard contract categories are generally used for all specialties.

Table 8.5 summarises the costing and pricing approach for 1994/95 contracts.

Table 8.5: 1994/95 pricing – case studies

	St Somewhere Trust	Thereabouts Unit
Cost attribution	Multi-staged approach, except for 2 per cent uplift to specialty costs for general (remote) overheads	Two-staged approach. No % uplift to specialty costs for remote overheads, some support service costs (as permitted under NHSME guidance) apportioned direct to specialties
Cost analysis	All purchasers with contracts – GPFH procedures priced separately with rest of work at average specialty price. 15 per cent on above prices for ECRs	Followed NHSME guidance but did not translate budgets into uniform categories
Cost type	• Overhead • Indirect • Direct (and capital charges) Local interpretation, especially regarding overhead	• Overhead • Indirect • Direct (and capital charges) Followed NHSME guidance but did not translate budgets into uniform categories
Contract categories	DHAs – specialties GPFHs – procedures ECRs – banded procedures (major, intermediate and minor)	All purchasers with contracts: GPFH procedures priced separately with rest of work at average specialty price. 15 per cent on above prices for ECRs

8.5 Summary

The case studies have shown how marked differences in costing approaches for pricing contracts remain. A number of factors influence the costing and pricing process which reduce the impact of the NHSME's endeavours to achieve uniform approaches to costing and pricing. Past experience affects how the guidance is applied and information needed for budgetary control and decision-making inevitably takes precedence over guidance set down by a remote Executive. Lack of consistency in both the costing process and how those costs are compiled into product lines will make comparative efficiency very difficult to assess.

Price comparisons and accounting choices are discussed in the next chapter.

9
The Case Studies – Pricing and Accounting Choices

9.1 Introduction

This chapter firstly compares the prices in the case studies to illustrate some of the difficulties facing purchasers in attempting to make efficient purchasing decisions. The extent of price manipulation and cost-shifting in the case studies is examined. Finally, the problems of efficient cost-based pricing are discussed in terms of the accounting choices facing healthcare providers.

9.2 Comparison of the 'published' prices

The two cases used different definitions of service ('product lines') for pricing purposes, and at St Somewhere there was a different pricing system for different types of purchaser. Hence meaningful price comparisons are often difficult. Indeed, if price depends on the type of purchaser, rather than the service provided, prices surely cannot provide appropriate 'efficiency' signals. Some broad comparisons of the prices for 1994/95 contracts are made below.

Table 9.1 provides comparisons of:

- average specialty prices used for DHAs (some specialties are excluded as average specialty prices were not published);
- the cost analysis and classification of the above specialties;
- some procedure prices and their associated average length of stay.

The average specialty prices (Table 9.1a) show St Somewhere to be relatively expensive for general surgery in-patient FCEs (though not day cases); oral surgery; paediatrics; and gynaecology. On the other hand, Thereabouts is more expensive for ENT and obstetrics, and the special care baby unit (SCBU) is three times more expensive.

Table 9.1: Case studies – price and cost analysis comparisons 1994/95

(a) *Average specialty prices*

	In-patient FCE £		Day cases £	
Specialty	*St Somewhere*[1]	*Thereabouts*[2]	*St Somewhere*[1]	*Thereabouts*[2]
General surgery	1,140	868	175	265
Oral surgery	806	660	510	385
Paediatrics	944	624	–	260
ENT	787	1,236	165	300
Gynaecology	687	346	227	233
Obstetrics	649	704	–	–
SCBU	1,192	3,484	–	–

Notes:
1 all procedures
2 excluding 97 GPFH procedures

(b) *Cost classification and analysis*

	Cost classification Var:semi-fixed:fixed (%)		Cost analysis Direct:indirect:overhead (%)	
Specialty	*St Somewhere*	*Thereabouts*	*St Somewhere*	*Thereabouts*
General surgery	17 – 66 – 17	23 – 68 – 9	40 – 58 – 2	48 – 24 – 28
Oral surgery	59 – 5 – 36	26 – 67 – 7	35 – 63 – 2	55 – 17 – 28
Paediatrics	13 – 78 – 9	24 – 69 – 7	46 – 52 – 2	60 – 14 – 26
ENT	27 – 56 – 17	29 – 68 – 3	44- 54 – 2	58 – 9 – 33
Gynaecology	13 – 72 – 15	31 – 61 – 8	37 – 61 – 2	48 – 18 – 34
Obstetrics	20 – 73 – 7	19 – 75 – 6	58 – 40 – 2	63 – 12 – 25
SCBU	n/a	25 – 70 – 5	93 – 5 – 2	63 – 11 – 26

(c) *Selected procedure prices and average length of stay (ALOS)*

Specialty	Procedure	St Somewhere Price £	ALOS	Thereabouts Price £	ALOS
Ophthalmology	Glaucoma	1,272 to 1,336	4	785	2.7
	Cataract	1,179 to 1,215	3	850	1.9
	Corneal	1,537	4	1,426	4.2
Gynaecology	D and C	341	1.34	312	1
	Hysterectomy	1,324	7	1,248	7.1
Orthopaedics	Hip	Total 4,465	17	Single 2,656	10
		Revision 6,623	16	Both 3,783	10
	Knee	Total 6,116	17	Single 2,756	10
		Revision 7,781	18	Both 3,983	10

The cost classification and analysis provided by the two case studies (Table 9.1b) sheds little light on these variations. With the exception of oral surgery, Thereabouts consistently classified more expenditure as variable; St Somewhere consistently used the overhead classification merely for the 2 per cent on cost for core management costs and classified the bulk of its costs as indirect. However, the SCBU at St Somewhere bears very little non-direct costs, i.e. 7 per cent compared with 37 per cent at Thereabouts.

Specialty prices between the two providers may consist of markedly different case mix. Indeed, the above comparisons will certainly be distorted by case-mix variations as Thereabouts removes the GPFH procedures from the specialty cost and calculates a specialty price for the balance.

Taking the procedures by specialty grouping the following observations can be made.

Ophthalmology

All ophthalmology procedures are cheaper at Thereabouts Unit on either an in-patient or a day-case basis. Thereabouts also has a shorter length of stay for those procedures where data is provided.

ENT

This specialty is much more expensive at Thereabouts. Thereabouts has a higher day rate – for example, 'lesion of nasal mucosa' is £166 as a day case at St Somewhere compared with £310 at Thereabouts. St Somewhere also has greater availability of day-case treatment: tonsillectomy, adenoidectomy and pharyngoscopy are all only available on a day-case basis at St Somewhere, but require an in-patient stay at Thereabouts. Indeed, a pharyngoscopy requires an average in-patient stay of 2.6 days at Thereabouts. Thereabouts also has longer stays for in-patient procedures, e.g. polypectomy requires 1.95 days at St Somewhere compared with 2.3 at Thereabouts.

General surgery

Day cases and in-patient procedures are priced higher at Thereabouts (despite cost-shifting detailed in section 9.3).

Urology

In-patient procedures are cheaper at Thereabouts, but day-case treatment is higher (see section 9.3 below).

Gynaecology

In-patient procedures are more expensive at Thereabouts despite similar lengths of stay (and some cost-shifting, section 9.3). Day cases are also more expensive, often twice as expensive (e.g. patency test, D and C, Bartholin's cyst).

Orthopaedics

Price comparisons between the two providers show no general pattern apart from day-case treatment being more expensive at Thereabouts. Some procedures are vastly more expensive at Thereabouts (e.g. trigger finger £330 at St Somewhere and £888 at Thereabouts), but others are much cheaper at Thereabouts (e.g. puncture of joint intra-articular aspiration £1047 at St Somewhere and £395 at Thereabouts). Even at GPFH procedure level comparisons are difficult as the providers subdivide procedures in different ways (see Table 9.1c). It would appear that the two providers may have quite different treatment regimes in this specialty.

Examining the cost analysis and classification of the two providers by specialty adds little to the above comparisons.

For the 1995/96 contracting process all providers were instructed to cost healthcare resource groups (HRGs) in either ophthalmology, gynaecology or orthopaedics (*NHS Executive*, 1994a). Both providers already priced some of these procedures separately for non-GPFHs; these are compared together with the associated ALOS (average length of stay) in Table 9.1c. The ALOS appears to be a much more meaningful indicator of price (and efficiency) differences than information derived from the NHSME prescribed cost analysis and classification. Moreover, it can be related appropriately to a clearly defined level of service, i.e. a treatment procedure.

9.3 Cost-shifting or price manipulation

At both providers, the cost-based prices were subject to some manipulation or massaging after compilation of draft prices.

St Somewhere

At St Somewhere, the Director of Finance and Contracting examined the effect of the initial prices on purchasers: DHAs and GPFHs.

DHAs

When it was found that the host DHA would be asked to pay 10 per cent more for the same activity than the previous year, adjustments were made. When the prices were issued, no individual DHA was expected to pay more than 1 per cent above 1993/94 contract income (before inflation adjustments). The DHAs receive their moneys on a weighted capitation basis and must live within their allocation. If St Somewhere had increased the charge for work performed for its host DHA, the DHA would have had to reduce the level of work purchased. St Somewhere would find it extremely difficult to maintain its activity levels through increased work from more distant DHAs even if their contract prices had reduced. This form of action would explain why few variations in purchaser contract income were reported by providers in the survey despite the majority stating that the NHSME's guidance had required substantial changes to their costing for pricing systems.

GPFHs

The 1993/94 GPFH contracts were on a cost per case basis. In order to encourage existing GPFHs and fourth-wave GPFHs to commence cost and volume contracts, a sliding scale of prices (Table 9.2) has been introduced.

Table 9.2: St Somewhere Trust – sliding scale of prices for GPFH

% of 1993/94 activity committed	% of published GPFH prices
No committed level	100
50% < 80% of budgeted activity	90
80% < 100% of budgeted activity	60
100% or over	30

The breakeven position is calculated to be at 103 per cent of budgeted activity. Therefore if GPFHs do not refer patients to St Somewhere as planned, there will be an under-recovery of cost on GPFH procedures. Some cross-subsidisation will arise according to the level of contract placed both between GPFHs and between GPFHs as a whole and DHAs. However, it is apparent that cross-subsidies between different types of purchaser would have arisen even without such sliding scales as GPFHs contract for work using different contract categories from DHAs, i.e. procedures as opposed to average specialty or banded procedures.

Thereabouts Unit

The Thereabouts Unit had declared at the outset of the costing process that GPFH prices were to be competitive. The Financial Controller issued the draft prices at a senior managers' meeting. Discussions ensued on the following service prices.

Surgery and urology

The surgery consultants asked that prices be kept to last year's level. This was achieved by adjusting the draft cost-based price. For example:

GPFH procedure 54: Ingrowing toenail	£
2 days @ £137	274
17 mins theatre @ £8.15	139
Total cost	413
Adjustment to 1993/94 price	(138)
Published price 1994/95	275

Thus the published price for this procedure was two-thirds of cost.

This manipulation was undertaken on the vast majority of surgery procedures with a compensating effect on average surgery prices for non-GPFH procedures. Similarly, prices for out-patient procedures were contrived to be below 1993/94 levels.

Gynaecology

Prices for GPFH procedures were adjusted, as above, to keep them competitive.

Paediatrics

Prices were 26 per cent higher than in 1993/94, but this was considered justified as a new paediatrics ward had been opened. (Paediatrics in 1994/95 were only 66 per cent of the price at St Somewhere.)

General medicine and age care

The price of general medicine had reduced from 1993/94 but age care had risen. The general manager suggested pricing as one product line and cross-subsidising. The business manager for the directorate consulted with the clinicians who decided that they wished to continue to price separately. However, within general medicine some out-patient cost was shifted to in-patient as the out-patient cost was higher than the previous year.

Both providers adjusted their cost-based pricing significantly. However, both felt that the cost-shifting would not be detected by the auditors or, even if it was, that it could be justified. Even though the NHS Executive stipulates cost assignment in some detail, it is difficult to query cost attribution by on-the-spot managers. Also, while cost attribution may be prescribed, there appears little guidance or control over the estimated activity or workload used in the costing models although these have an important impact on cost-based prices.

9.4 Accounting choices and efficient pricing

In the first four years of the market, prices were not providing appropriate signals to facilitate the market's efficiency aims. Prices were neither reasonable measures of resource consumption nor capable of being compared meaningfully between alternative providers. Whether accounting choices can be made to enable prices to produce the necessary price signals is considered below.

The elusive true cost

It is extremely difficult to achieve reliable costs because of the individual nature of healthcare provision. This appears to be a common problem of service industries, which could explain why cost-based pricing is not prevalent for services. *Fitzgerald et al.* (1991) noted:

> *'When we looked at a range of service companies we were surprised to find that many of them did not seem to try to accurately cost individual services, either to ascertain their profitability or to set prices. This may be explained by the difficulty many of them had in tracing costs.'*
> *Fitzgerald et al.* (1991)

They go on to observe that costing has been used extensively to plan and control via responsibility centres (an observation that is equally applicable to the NHS, section 5.3), but conclude:

> *'Costs are not extensively used to make price decisions in service industries except in professional services.'* *Fitzgerald et al.* (1991)

The 'true' cost of healthcare services is an elusive concept. The Brunel study of the resource management pilot sites found that validity of information was difficult to achieve, but the linking of costs and activity depends on having accurate activity information available (*Packwood et al.*, 1991). In Chapter 3 it was illustrated how the full cost could be derived in a number of different ways. Given the high level of indirect and overhead costs and the vast range of services provided by acute hospitals, the full cost of individual healthcare services cannot be determined with precision. This problem is compounded as the cost object is more closely defined (e.g. from broad specialty to specific procedures within specialty). At specialty level, a large proportion of costs are direct: clinicians, nurses, ward clerks, etc. As the cost objective moves below specialty level to procedures, very few direct costs can be identified: 'direct treatment services' are subject to apportionment. *Cooper* (1990) describes the hierarchical 'resource consumption' model which explains that the lower one attempts to compile full costs, the greater the need for arbitrary allocations and apportionments.

In recent years there has been considerable debate and development on how to generate product costs. The debate stems from the activity-based costing (ABC) method originally developed in a manufacturing context. It is argued that an ABC approach will result in more accurate product costs (*Cooper and Kaplan*, 1988). An ABC approach has been considered to be appropriate to product costing in healthcare (*HFMA/KPMG*, 1992; *Chan*, 1993; *CIMA*, 1993; *King et al.*, 1994).

On the introduction of the NHS internal market, many overheads and indirect costs were applied direct to contracts on an in-patient day basis. The NHSME *Costing for Contracting Manual* currently recommends this approach for catering, laundry and portering services; and after specialty costs have been compiled, in-patient days are largely used to determine procedure costs. High in-patient day rates make bed days, at least apparently, an extremely expensive resource, and therefore operating practice has been continually modified to reduce bed days (which intensifies the effect of high day rates because the costs are artificial). An ABC approach would examine the nature of overheads and their causes. Cost drivers would then be applied to cost output.

Chan (1993) and *CIMA* (1993) considered the use of ABC to build up unique patient costs (similar to the patient costing in the RM initiative). *HFMA/ KPMG* (1992) and *King et al.* (1994) considered ABC product costing potential in relation to costing contract categories. The *Costing for Contracting Manual* specifies one base for apportionment of each department's cost, while twelve bases are specified for apportioning overhead or support service departments (i.e. non-patient treatment departments). In examining specific areas of hospital cost, more than one cost driver is usually appropriate. For example, theatre costs are attributed according to operating time in the *Costing for Contracting Manual*, but there are at least two factors (the number of operations and the length of operation) which drive theatre costs. In the case studies, the costs were attributed in greater detail than specified in the *Manual*. Individual budget lines were often input rather than the total budgeted cost of the department, and a number of different apportionment bases were used. In this respect it could be argued that elements of the ABC approach are already apparent in NHS costing practice. Admittedly, in the case studies, the budgets were not assigned to homogeneous cost pools, but the development of costing below specialty level does recommend the use of a number of homogeneous cost pools designated as condition-specific or time-based and as variable, semi-fixed and fixed.

Theoretically, the greater use of the ABC approach could lead to costs and hence prices which closely reflected resource consumption. However, there are two practical impediments to the development of more sophisticated approaches to healthcare product costing:

(a) The costs associated with sophisticated systems. Set-up and operating costs of an ABC system may be high owing to the complex technical nature of much of the work (*King et al.*, 1994; *HFMA/ KPMG*, 1992). The 1994 survey highlighted the investment in resource activity systems necessary for more sophisticated systems. *King et al.* also indicate high costs in consultant fees, staff time and behavioural impact. A recent HFMA report estimated that the NHS Executive's *further* costing initiative may cost over £10m without taking account of the extra activity information required in operational departments (*Brown*, 1995).

(b) The limited use made of more sophisticated cost information (see section 9.3 and section 10.2). The accountants in the case studies saw the cost-based prices as a starting point for contract negotiation. In the cost-shifting undertaken for pricing purposes, the accountants in both case studies foresaw no difficulty in the audit scrutiny of the costing process. They felt that nobody could claim to be more knowledgeable than the manager on the spot about how the costs related to specialties and/or procedures.

There was little evidence of demand for more sophisticated costing or pricing. These findings are reinforced by *King et al.* (1994):

> *'There was a feeling evident, particularly among business managers, that more sophisticated treatment costs were not necessary. In part this was considered due to the need to use only broadly based costs in*

> *contract planning as the whole exercise was subject to great uncertainty. Moreover, there was some evidence that the main customers, HAs, were not demanding and could not cope with more extensive and detailed costings.'*

The use of more accurate costing methods such as ABC would be justified only where the expected benefits outweigh the expected costs; simple approaches may be 'optimal' when information costs are introduced into the frame. The benefits of more accurate information for product pricing in the NHS internal market may not be significant, but the benefits of ABC are now largely seen in terms of cost management as it is activities rather than costs which can be managed (*Brimson*, 1991; *Cooper and Kaplan*, 1992; *Johnson*, 1988).

The comparative true cost

Obtaining costs which are reasonably accurate *and comparable* is even more problematic. In order for purchasers to make rational decisions between providers, they must be able to make valid price comparisons. However, the 1994 survey shows significant differences in cost attribution methods and apportionment bases. The case studies highlight this latter point and also explain some of the reasons for nonconformity. The two case study providers continue to have markedly different approaches to the cost attribution processes. This is inevitable as the NHSME is specifying a minimum approach above which providers are encouraged to develop, and setting the guidance using summary headings when most providers are compiling cost flows on a much more detailed basis.

Presumably, the NHSME's encouragement of costing for pricing above its prescribed minimum level is to enable the costs compiled to move closer to the elusive 'true' cost. *Sutcliffe* (1991) has illustrated the possibility of aggregation effects if departments are merged for service cost allocation. As costing approaches become more complex (and accurate) they will also be harder to standardise. *King et al.* (1994) found that an ABC study of the radiology service would have to be modified for use in other hospitals. Studies concerning cost allocation techniques suggest that accounting methods used in practice are 'driven' by political, behavioural and organisational control factors rather than economic ones (*Atkinson*, 1987). In the case studies it was found that the need to achieve 'ownership' of data and be in congruence with budget systems was more important than guidance by the NHSME. As *Bromwich and Bhimani* (1989) observe:

> *'No isolated search for more effective cost allocation methods within a constrained theoretical economic framework is likely to yield universal guides to managerial issues of cost management.'*

Similarly, the cost analysis and classification laid down by the NHSME is not applied consistently, consequently adding little to comparisons between providers.

The major problem in comparing prices and costs between alternative providers is the lack of a commonly defined product or standard contract category. HRGs are currently being adopted to inform the contracting process, but as costing becomes more detailed and complex it also becomes more costly and difficult to ensure a uniform approach. If providers become more sophisticated in an unco-ordinated manner, this in itself may lead to distortions in resource allocation – provider prices for some services will be cheaper (or more expensive) merely because of the lower product level used by individual providers if development of more sophisticated pricing develops in an unco-ordinated manner. There is a conflict between accuracy and comparability, but both must be achieved in order to provide appropriate price signals. The benefits from more accurate cost systems are largely in terms of cost management, but this requires cost systems to be tailored to individual circumstances (political, behavioural and organisational considerations). On the other hand, the individual tailoring of cost systems impedes consistency and hence comparability. Furthermore, providers need to develop in unison if misallocations are to be avoided.

The conditional true cost

It has long been accepted in accounting literature that cost depends on the purpose for which it is to be used. *Clarke* (1923) concluded that there could be no unique concept of cost. *Piper and Wally* (1990, 1991) have argued that a more complicated product costing system is not necessarily a more accurate or useful one. The accuracy of ABC, they argue, assumes that increasing the number of cost drivers improves accuracy, but not all overheads behave linearly in respect of a cost driver. A conditional truth approach requires relevance not accuracy.

The NHS costing for pricing principles stipulate a full absorption cost, including current cost depreciation and a return on capital, for pricing purposes; marginal cost is permitted only for in-year unplanned spare capacity. The high level of fixed and semi-fixed costs in hospitals makes this a financially unattractive approach for many pricing decisions at individual provider level. This is particularly the case in healthcare, which is a multi-product service with economies of scale and scope. Full costs include apportionments of fixed costs which may be unaffected by particular contracts. In the case study sites, it made financial sense at local level to provide a sliding scale of prices to GP fundholders according to the level of work they committed to the trust. Similarly, cross-subsidisation of GPFH procedure prices at Thereabouts was also financially sound (there is a large volume of costs which are common (joint) for procedures within the specialty). Full-cost pricing may lead to work being lost which could provide a substantial contribution. The providers need cost systems which help them manage costs but, while to remain viable they must recover their costs, full-cost pricing of each area of work or for each purchaser may not be the provider's best financial strategy. (The debate concerning absorption or marginal cost for pricing purposes is covered in section 3.4.) The NHSME's rules are not in line with the financial incentives at local level.

The NHSME's guidance for a uniform analysis and classification of costs holds similar problems. Chapter 1 of the *Costing for Contracting Manual* stipulates:

> *'the contracting process would be more flexible and responsive to changes in activity if the proportion of costs identified as fixed were to be reduced and the proportion of costs identified as variable were to be increased.'*

This proposed movement is illustrated in Figure 9.1. The NHSME argues that changes in the structure of costs are necessary if providers are to become more flexible and responsive to changes in the pattern of demand.

Figure 9.1: Proposed movement in cost structure

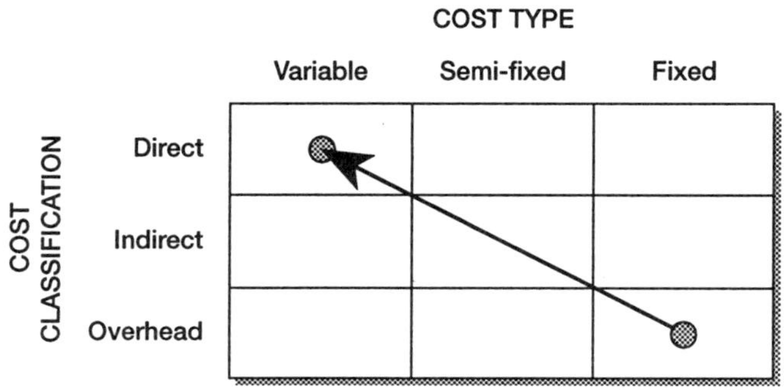

However, treating more costs as direct requires more detailed recording systems and this does not necessarily lead to benefits unless it will effect decisions. According to the pricing rules, it could reduce cross-subsidisation due to misallocation, but it would generate higher overall prices. On the other hand, the case studies indicate that it is market forces which lead to cost-shifting, and therefore increased precision would be futile (though arguably it may be harder to disguise such cost-shifting).

An imposed analysis of costs as variable, semi-fixed and fixed has little meaning to individual providers. Classifying an element of cost as variable does not alter the behaviour of that cost element – the behaviour will be determined by the particular circumstances at each provider not by the tag assigned by the NHSME. Nursing costs are classified as semi-fixed in the guidance, but the hospital may be able to shift nursing resource flexibly between a number of specialties. It is this ability which is important rather than the length of the employment contract. In the multi-product NHS, flexibility in the use of resources is the real issue, and this will depend on local operational arrangements.

Local circumstances are likely to dictate the providers' pricing strategy and a form of useful cost analysis and classification. A number of writers have postulated how easy it would be to manipulate full-cost prices. *MacKerrell* (1993) observes that prices are normally determined by the market-place and are often not made on a full-cost basis at least in the short term:

> *'But how can a manager affect the result of a calculation when the method has been predetermined? Simply, the manager must select an*

> *appropriate basis for allocating indirect costs to individual procedures in order to arrive at a full cost.'*

Providers would be able to influence price through their methods of cost allocation and apportionment and activity estimation; freedom still remains despite the 1993 guidance (which makes no attempt to address activity estimation). *Mellet et al.* (1993) point out that providers could employ penetration pricing through underestimating costs and/ or overestimating activity or, conversely, price skimming by overestimating costs and/or underestimating volume, thereby exploiting their monopoly position for certain services. The case studies provide evidence of such action despite the 1993 guidance. Therefore, if the pricing rules are to produce accurate, full-cost prices constructed in a consistent manner, they must be obligatory and not merely guidance, very clearly and thoroughly set out and be capable of enforcement.

9.5 Summary

Price comparisons at present are fraught with difficulties. Often the service is so broadly defined or not defined consistently by providers, and therefore comparisons are not meaningful or even possible. The cost analysis and classification, as implemented, is unhelpful. Basic data regarding length of stay and outcomes seem much more reliable and relevant than inconsistent cost data. Price variances may still be due to differing cost approaches and, indeed, the instances of cost-shifting highlighted above question the basic premise that individual prices actually reflect cost. Cost-based prices are adjusted according to 'market conditions' – competitor prices and the ability of purchasers to pay.

Cost-based pricing has failed to provide appropriate price signals to purchasers in the first four years of the NHS internal market: prices neither accurately reflected resources consumed nor enabled valid price comparisons between providers. Examination of the accounting choices shows the search for accurate health service product costs to be technically difficult and expensive. The nature of healthcare services makes homogeneous products very difficult to determine, let alone their full cost in precise terms. There will be high transaction costs (additional activity systems, staff resources, etc.) associated with compiling such costs and prices and operating detailed contracts. When the further requirement of comparability is added, achievement of appropriate costs becomes still more problematic. There is conflict between accuracy and comparability. Accurate costing (and classification and analysis) should reflect local operational management and therefore rigid rules cannot apply. A further stumbling block is costing relevance. Although costly 'truth' could be achieved, and to some extent even costly 'comparable truth', the financial incentives at individual provider level are not consistent with full-cost pricing including a 6 per cent return for all 'products' and all purchasers. It has been shown that there will be incentives at individual provider level to cost-shift to manipulate prices. The nature of acute health service costs (i.e. the high level of joint costs and few direct costs), particularly at procedure level, make it relatively easy to manipulate cost-based prices. Therefore compliance with costing and pricing rules will be difficult to ensure.

10 Contract Negotiation and the Emerging Market

10.1 Introduction

This chapter considers contract negotiation in the two case studies and in the emerging NHS internal market. Firstly, the contract negotiation process is followed and the level of 'openness' in costing and pricing is established. The latter part uses the findings from the cases and the surveys to provide an analysis of the cost-based pricing rules in the context of the emerging NHS internal market.

10.2 Contract negotiation

In November, each provider was required to submit its prices for the forthcoming financial year to the regional health authority. The contract negotiation with purchasers (DHAs and GPFHs) was undertaken in the ensuing months.

St Somewhere Trust

At St Somewhere, the contracts are negotiated with the purchasers by a team: the Director of Finance and Contracting; Director of Marketing and Contracting; and the Director of Information and Corporate Planning. The clinical directors and business managers are not in attendance at contract negotiation meetings (except for the host DHA), but they are consulted on any changes to the contracts from the previous year and their agreement is required before contracts are finalised. Quality aspects are discussed, though often separate meetings are used to discuss the issues more fully.

The prices were calculated using estimated current year activity. As contracts are negotiated, analysis is undertaken showing movements from the baseline in terms of both activity and revenue. The movements are further analysed according to whether they relate to additional emergency work, switch from in-patient to day-case work and 'equilibrium', i.e. activity necessary to maintain waiting-time targets. Changes to the base activity level do not give rise to recalculation of prices through the costing and pricing model. Each purchaser was allowed 2.25 per cent additional activity at no extra cost as part of the Government's efficiency targets. Generally, other adjustments in activity would be negotiated at 30 per cent of full cost/ price. The trust continued with this approach for 1994/95 contracts despite the availability of the cost analysis which showed that variable costs by specialty at St Somewhere range from 7 per cent to 36 per cent or even higher in some regional specialties. However, one purchaser negotiated changes (increases and decreases) at full cost.

As shown in Table 9.2, in order to encourage existing GPFHs and fourth-wave GPFHs to commence cost and volume contracts, a sliding scale of prices was used in negotiations. The greater commitment and hence reduced risk associated with cost and volume contracts makes this type of contract attractive to the trust and is also administratively easier for both parties. However, such tactics are against the NHSME's rules and 'should not be undertaken' (*NHSME*, 1994b).

Thereabouts Unit

At Thereabouts Unit, the contract negotiation is undertaken by a team consisting of the Directors of Contracting, Finance, and Information Management. The Head of Nursing and Quality sometimes joins the team, but quality tends to be discussed at separate meetings.

The prices were calculated in the costing and pricing model using 1993/94 contracted activity. As the Director of Contracting explained:

> *'Price tends not to be a major negotiation issue, but the total contract value is!'*

Work above the costing model plus 2.25 per cent (efficiency target) is priced at 45 per cent of full cost/price:

> *'Pressure to reduce this margin is being experienced from the host DHA and some (more knowledgeable) GPFHs.'*

Thus a standard (but higher) percentage is used throughout contract negotiations. Variable costs at Thereabouts range, depending on specialty, from 3 to 9 per cent.

The contracts are relatively sophisticated in terms of workload and price analysis as Thereabouts uses GPFH procedure prices for all purchasers.

Thereabouts has experienced difficulties through pricing in a more sophisticated manner than neighbouring providers. One DHA wished to contract only for the cheaper procedures within each specialty and use another provider, which priced on an average specialty basis, for the other procedures. The existence of fixed costs (which are largely joint costs of procedures within a specialty) made the loss of part of the business disadvantageous to Thereabouts. Thereabouts therefore felt unable to negotiate a contract with this DHA. The DHA accounts for about 5 per cent of Thereabouts' total workload. This situation prompted Thereabouts to introduce an additional 15 per cent charge for extra contractual referrals (ECRs). Thereabouts argues that this represents the additional transaction cost associated with such referrals.

The host HA received a large increase in funding for 1994/95 due to a change in the formula used. The resultant additional work undertaken for the host HA will be treated as an additional contract 'to relieve waiting lists, etc.', and negotiated after the start of the year. By using this mechanism, the host HA will gain maximum benefit from the additional funds (if the costing model was rerun with the additional workload, the other purchasers would receive some of the gain from the spreading of the hospitals' fixed cost over a greater volume). A separate marginal costing exercise will be undertaken to cost the extra work for the host HA. The 45 per cent used in earlier years, and for other purchasers in 1994/95, is regarded as inadequate. Similarly, the cost analysis calculated under the NHSME guidance (variable, semi-fixed and fixed) is regarded as not sufficiently robust, especially as the host HA is likely to request a 10 per cent increase in their activity above the original pricing model.

Disclosure of cost and price information

Despite having analysed and classified costs according to NHSME guidance (direct, indirect and overhead; and variable, semi-fixed and fixed) this information was not made routinely available to purchasers by either case study provider.

The Thereabouts Unit provided extensive analysis of its budgets to its host DHA, but was not asked for the analysis and classification of costs under the NHSME guidance. The St Somewhere Trust provided the analysis and classification to its host purchaser towards the end of the contract negotiations. Both providers expressed a willingness to provide the information if requested. However, neither provider appeared to utilise the information in contract negotiations

St Somewhere Trust provides the following information to purchasers:

- prices by average specialty for DHAs, by GPFH procedure for GPFHs;
- existing purchasers received a contract analysis by specialty;
- GPFHs receive a marketing brochure and are informed via a bi-monthly newsletter of waiting times and lists by consultant.

The host DHA is issued information building up the trust's total quantum of cost together with a purchaser summary (this is available to others if requested).

Thereabouts Unit distributes the following information to purchasers:

- prices by GPFH procedure for all purchasers, and for DHAs the remaining workload by average specialty cost for that workload;
- a standard booklet on facilities and staff;
- contract monitoring report detailing base activity, budget and waiting list.

Extensive further information is issued to the host DHA:

> *'They go through the unit's quantum of cost with a fine-tooth comb!'*

As the Thereabouts Unit was directly managed by its host DHA until 1 April 1994, there had been considerable debate about the distribution of the costs of the DHA which related to the provider rather than to its purchasing role.

The case studies show openness in costing to be patchy. Information is more likely to be provided to the host purchaser, but at present little demand for the NHSME standard information is apparent. Negotiations centre on the total contract value rather than individual prices or cost structure.

Contracting timetable

Contract negotiation is mainly undertaken in the January to March preceding the financial year. DHAs appear unwilling to commence contract negotiations earlier, presumably because of uncertainty surrounding the funds available to them. In February 1994, fourth-wave GPFHs (i.e. GP practices becoming fundholders on 1 April 1994) received *draft* budget proposals and there was uncertainty surrounding earlier waves because of changes in their funding. Consequently, the amount of deduction from the DHAs' budget was also uncertain.

The NHSME directive states that all contracts should be signed before the start of the financial year. At 31 March 1994, both case study providers had a significant part of their anticipated contracts for 1994/95 still to be agreed. At St Somewhere Trust, 72 per cent of anticipated contract income had been agreed, but GPFH contracts (6 per cent) and contracts for regional specialty work (20 per cent) were still outstanding. At Thereabouts Unit approximately 78 per cent of anticipated contract income had been agreed, but contracts with GPFHs and some DHAs were outstanding. Indeed, Thereabouts Unit had never finalised the 1993/94 contract with its second-largest purchaser (10 per cent of contract income). However, there is a three-year contract in operation with this purchaser which guarantees a minimum of £2.24m per annum before inflation adjustments.

The *Audit Commission* (1993) has noted the general problem that contracts remain unsigned well into the financial year:

> *'A vicious circle of uncertainty can sometimes develop with providers unwilling to quote prices until they know precisely what level of work to expect, and purchasers unable to commit themselves to a level of activity until they have prices from each provider.'*

10.3 The emerging NHS internal market

Cost-based pricing in the internal market model

Quasi- or internal markets operate via a price mechanism. The NHS internal market was clearly established to improve the efficiency of the NHS. It has been shown (Chapter 2) that if perfect competition (or perfect contestability) existed, these efficiency aims could be achieved without price regulation. Competition would be real, and purchasers would use alternative (potential) suppliers if prices were above the efficient level. However, at least in the early years, the NHS internal market could be subject to abuse by monopoly providers not operating in a contestable market. The DoH's chosen price mechanism, i.e. full-cost pricing including a 6 per cent real return on the current replacement cost of capital and no planned cross-subsidisation, sought to imitate the 'ideal hospital market' (*DoH*, 1989f). Prices were to be based on LRAC which, as the DoH argues that there are no economies of scale in district general hospitals with more than 600 beds, will generally equate to LRMC. To prevent the abuse of monopoly power through cost-enhancing inefficiency, openness in costing was seen as necessary to provide yardstick competition where real competition could not occur. The abuse of monopoly power, it was envisaged, would also be curbed by monopsony power (*Bryan and Beech*, 1991).

Market structure and operation

As described in section 7.5, the NHS internal market is made up of a reducing number of larger purchasers and providers. *Butler* (1992) forewarns of such developments that there is:

> *'a natural tendency for oligopolies to form in a market dominated by block contracts ... [and this] ... might be unnaturally enhanced by the providers themselves. Competition is not the inevitable consequence of a market environment: providers might seek to preserve their interests just as much by collaborating with each other as by engaging in competition.'*
>
> *Butler* (1992)

The perfectly competitive model of neo-classical economics was at odds with NHS healthcare provision at the inception of the market (Figure 3.1) and has become even more so as the market has developed. The market for GPFH procedures (particularly in the large conurbations) is the most competitive. In both case studies pressure to keep GPFH prices competitive was experienced. However, this did not lead to pricing at LRAC, but rather cost-shifting to other less competitive contracts. There is evidence of cross-subsidisation between products and purchasers.

The case studies also provide evidence of monopsony power. An example is the cost shifting by purchaser undertaken at St Somewhere (section 8.6) which led to 1994/95 base contracts being within 1 per cent of 1994/95 contracts; another is the treatment of the host DHA's additional funding at Thereabouts. The little change in total contract value, as identified in the 1994 survey, for each DHA may also indicate similar relationships, given that most providers regarded the changes to their costing approach as substantial following the NHSME guidance. While monopsony power may constrain providers, it may also operate to the detriment of other, less-powerful purchasers.

In practice, many markets are observed to operate not by the economist's 'invisible hand', but by what a former chairman of the President's Council of Economic Advisors in the USA labelled the 'invisible handshake' (*Okun*, 1981). By this, Okun means that routine and automatic price arrangements are often agreed upon in order to create continuity and convenience of supply. Consequently, prices become 'sticky' and do not directly reflect shifts in market conditions. This is what appears to be happening in the NHS internal market: the market is a set of oligopolies and oligopsonies in which inter-institutional bargaining is the central mechanism by which resources are allocated. Firms succeed by the (essentially non-competitive) relations they build. This also appears to be the reality of organisations in the present NHS internal market: purchasers are price negotiators, not price takers.

In the NHS internal market model, openness in costing was seen as providing a stimulus to provider efficiency (section 3.4). Such openness would enable contract negotiators to spot potential abuse of monopoly and monopsony power and to highlight the existence of differences in efficiency (*DoH*, 1989f). However, to make meaningful assessments of cost some uniformity of approach is required. Openness in costing is less meaningful without some consistency in terms of the contract category or product line. The standard classification and analysis of costs by behaviour and type are not easily applied consistently and are extremely broad classifications.

Both the 1994 survey and the case studies show that the classification and analysis was subject to differing interpretation. Furthermore, disclosure is not obligatory and the NHSME's existing stance on openness is ambivalent. The NHSME states in the foreword to the *Costing Manual* that it 'feels strongly that there is a need for greater openness in contracting between purchasers and providers than currently characterises the contracting process', but then in the guidance documentation goes on to scramble the cost data from the pilot site 'so as not to reveal detailed costing data confidential to the pilot study unit'!

The case studies, and to some extent the 1994 survey, have shown that the emerging NHS market(s) does not resemble the model espoused on the introduction of the NHS internal market, i.e. purchasers observing the prices charged by several providers for a particular product and selecting the lowest-price provider as the one with which to agree a contract. The picture is more akin to industry models where contracts are negotiated between a few buyers and sellers on terms that are not made known to other potential purchasers or providers. The prices are a starting point for negotiations. *Dawson* (1994) draws the analogy with industries where product prices are posted (textiles, paper):

> '*Published price lists exist* either *for small buyers not sufficiently important for the supplier to cultivate,* or *as a starting point for price negotiation. Neither buyer nor seller has an interest in negotiated prices becoming public knowledge.*' *Dawson* (1994)

In this environment attempts to establish either meaningful cost-based prices or openness in costing and pricing will be extremely difficult.

The NHSME's rules impose a system of pricing contrary to the market structure for acute health services. This is not surprising. The rules were devised because of difficulties in ensuring competitive or contestable markets; however, in the emerging market, compliance with such rules will be difficult to enforce. The case studies and the surveys have shown that cost-based pricing rules permit subjectivity and can easily be manipulated. Furthermore, openness in costing and pricing to achieve yardstick competition is also at odds with current market operation.

Transaction costs and the competitive market

In Chapter 2, the transaction cost approach was used to justify the use of non-market structures. In the NHS internal market, the pricing rules had been devised in an attempt to overcome problems relating to the abuse of monopoly power. However, markets may be inappropriate not just through failings evident in neo-classical economics. Markets and the price mechanism may be inefficient because of the existence of high transaction costs in operating the market. In situations that involve uncertainty, bounded rationality and opportunism, it is important to economise on resources used in negotiating, implementing and adapting contracts. This is what appears to be happening in the NHS internal market.

Uncertainty

The unpredictable nature of healthcare (especially for non-elective work) means that cost per case contracts are very risky for both the purchaser and the provider. Relating prices to activity is seen as fundamental in using market mechanisms to encourage economic efficiency. Without it, purchasers cannot make rational choices between providers and providers will still be impeded in their attempts to become more efficient because of the 'efficiency trap' (section 3.2). In 1991/92, according to the 1991 survey, 89 per cent of hospital income was from block contracts, 8 per cent from cost and volume contracts and 3 per cent cost per case. By 1994, some progress towards contracts related more closely to activity was apparent, but block contracts still accounted for 84 per cent of contract income. Both case studies used block contracts with DHAs; such contracts accounted for 76 per cent or 88 per cent of total contract and ECR income. Under uncertainty, contracts become very complex and costly to enforce. This would explain the continued reliance on block contracts after four years of the NHS internal market.

Bounded rationality

The extremely high level of detail necessary to place all contracts on a procedure basis (there are nearly 500 HRGs and over 10,000 ICD9/OPCS codes) places limits on both purchasers and providers, but contracts at specialty level provide very imprecise service definition. Cost per case contracts at procedure level would be even more daunting.

There are indications that purchasers are unable or unwilling to cope with more detailed contracting (little demand for more sophisticated information, concern over total contract value rather than price per item, etc.). The considerable transaction costs may indicate the reluctance to pursue more detailed contracts. There is little incentive to use more sophisticated costing and pricing from either the purchaser or provider perspective. For the provider, more accurate costing is more expensive and it was unlikely to change the contract prices as these were related to competitive GPFH prices or the DHA ability to pay. From the purchaser perspective, more accurate costing is also more expensive (i.e. provider costs are recovered from purchasers) and as each host DHA is often purchasing the vast majority of its local provider's services, it has little to gain by reducing errors of apportionment (though much to gain by reducing errors of magnitude). It would appear that price is not a major factor influencing purchaser decisions. An *NAHAT* (1993) survey found that existing patient flows, GP-expressed preference, previous experience of providers, and ease of travel for residents were all given greater weight in influencing decisions about where to place contracts in 1992/93 than competitive prices. For both parties, transaction costs increase as contracts become more detailed both in terms of activity (i.e. movement from block to cost and volume or cost per case contracts) and product grouping (i.e. from broad specialty to defined procedures).

Opportunistic behaviour

When services are only loosely defined within block contracts, there is scope for opportunistic behaviour, e.g. a provider treating less-complex cases or not providing care which leads to efficient outcomes. In order to overcome this within a market approach, costly medical audit or performance review may be needed which again is costly to administer. However, more co-operative modes of governance may be able to achieve adherence to objectives without such costly mechanisms.

The problems are exacerbated by 'small numbers' and 'asset specificity'. The research has shown that increasingly small numbers (with the exception of GPFHs) of purchasers and providers are operating in the NHS internal market. There are therefore few or no alternatives open for a buyer or a seller to replace each other in a transaction. The cost-shifting between purchasers at St Somewhere following the costing for pricing exercise could be regarded as indicative of the lack of alternative purchasers. Similarly, purchasers are locked in to providers because of asset specificity resulting from the geographic location, the loyalty of GPs to existing referral patterns, etc. The high asset specificity leads to the parties being dependent on each other and the costs of switching contracts prohibitive.

High transaction costs appear to have impeded the development of the NHS internal market. The former mode of governance in the NHS was bureaucratic. Within these governance structures, rules or traditions drive performance rather than prices. The developing internal market appears not to be mimicking the neo-classical market model, but following a more co-operative, network model. Long-term relationships have an important influence on NHS contracting.

10.4 Summary

After prices have been 'published' they are not set in tablets of stone, but merely form the basis of negotiated contracts. Purchasers are able to influence the total contract value and consequently the prices for work performed. The providers operate differing pricing arrangements for different purchasers. Openness in costing appears patchy. Information is more likely to be provided to the host purchaser, but at present little demand for the NHSME standard information is apparent. Negotiations centre on the total contract value rather than individual prices or cost structure. The contracts are loosely defined and are linked to long-term relations.

The NHSME rules are a necessary attempt to try to achieve consistent, meaningful and comparable prices to enable purchasers to make efficient choices. However, in the emerging market, the prescribed pricing regime seems out of step with the way contracts are actually negotiated and relationships maintained. The pricing regime relates to a model where purchasers observe the prices charged by several providers for a particular product and select the lowest-price provider (i.e. the retail model). The reality appears to be a much more co-operative, network arrangement which is akin to many industrial markets and can be explained by transaction cost economics. Contracts are negotiated and long-term relations developed. Market incentives do not exist to ensure that economic efficiency through the price mechanism is facilitated.

11 Conclusion

11.1 Introduction

In this final chapter the implications of the research are highlighted and the further development of cost-based pricing discussed. Finally, the main research conclusions are set out.

11.2 Implications and the further development of cost-based pricing

Implications of the research findings

The basic conditions set out for appropriate price signals and the operation of the market (Figure 1.1) are not observed and serious problems surround their future achievement. The NHS pricing principles and guidance were established to simulate the pricing in a perfectly competitive market and avoid the abuse of monopoly power.

Cost-based pricing has failed to provide appropriate price signals to purchasers in the first five years of the internal market; prices neither accurately reflect resources consumed, nor enable valid price comparisons between providers to be made. In 1991, improved contract categories, consistency of approach and bases of cost attribution were required to facilitate economic efficiency. Three years later, the cost methods behind the prices had improved and the 1993 NHSME guidance had led to increased consistency, but there were examples of non-compliance and there was much local subjectivity concerning application of the guidance. There is still a lack of activity systems to enable even some direct patient care costs to be accurately attributed to specialties and, most importantly, to enable more meaningful, consistent contract categories to be used below specialty level. The vast bulk of provider income is still derived from block contracts.

Price comparisons are difficult. Services are often too broadly defined or not defined consistently, and therefore price comparisons are not meaningful or even possible. The cost analysis and classification stipulated in the NHSME guidance, as implemented, is unhelpful. Basic data regarding length of stay and outcomes seems much more reliable and relevant than inconsistent cost data. Price variances may be due to differing cost approaches and, indeed, the instances of cost-shifting found in the case studies question the basic premise that individual prices actually reflect cost. Cost-based prices are adjusted according to 'market conditions' – competitor prices and the ability of purchasers to pay.

Examination of the accounting choices shows the search for accurate health service product costs to be technically difficult and expensive. The nature of healthcare services makes homogeneous products very difficult to determine, let alone their full cost, in precise terms. There will be high transaction costs associated with compiling such costs and prices and operating detailed contracts. When the further requirement of comparability is added, achievement of appropriate costs becomes even more problematic. There is conflict between accuracy and comparability. Accurate costing (and classification and analysis) should reflect local operational management and therefore rigid rules cannot apply.

A further stumbling block is costing relevance. It has been shown that there will be incentives at individual provider level to cost-shift to manipulate prices. The nature of acute health service costs (i.e. the high level of joint costs and few direct costs), particularly at procedure level, makes it relatively easy to manipulate cost-based prices. Compliance with costing and pricing rules will therefore be difficult to ensure.

Openness in costing appears patchy; information is more likely to be provided to the host DHA but at present little demand for the NHSME standard classification and analysis of costs is apparent. Negotiations centre on total contract value rather than on individual prices or cost structure. The contracts are loosely defined and are linked to long-term relations.

The NHSME detailed guidance sought to achieve consistent, meaningful and comparable prices to enable purchasers to place contracts with efficient providers. However, in the emerging NHS internal market, the cost-based pricing rules seem out of step with the way contracts are actually negotiated and relationships maintained. The different perceptions of costing for pricing between the NHS Executive and individual providers is summarised in Figure 11.1. The cost-based pricing regime relates to a model where purchasers observe the prices charged by several providers for a particular product and select the lowest-price provider. The reality appears to be a much more co-operative network arrangement similar to that found in many industrial markets. Contracts are negotiated and long-term relationships developed. Appropriate market incentives do not exist to ensure that economic efficiency is facilitated through the price mechanism.

Figure 11.1: Different perceptions of costing for pricing

Costing for contracting rules: NHSME	*Individual trust or unit*
One 'true' or acceptable cost	Full cost is imprecise. Sophisticated cost systems are expensive and little needed for pricing purposes
Comparable cost: uniform allocation and apportionment; uniform cost analysis and classification	Local circumstances: budget structures ownership by managers/clinicians
Attribute all costs and a 6 per cent return on capital. No cross-subsidisation	Use relevant costs Consider decision or purpose
Standard contract categories	Local need. Product and purchaser differentiation
Openness in costing	Confidential/commercially sensitive

The further development of NHS pricing

For the 1995/96 contracting roun d, acute healthcare providers were required to cost HRGs in at least one specialty (ophthalmology, gynaecology or orthopaedics) to 'inform the contracting process'. The process was extended to the costing of HRGs in six specialties for the 1996/97 contracting round. However, as yet, HRG costs appear to have led neither to a common contracting 'currency' nor influenced contracting significantly.

At Thereabouts NHST, the HRG costs were not available in the chosen specialty, orthopaedics, until after the start of the contract year. Thereabouts continued to identify and price GPFH procedure treatments in its contracts with both DHAs and GPFHs. At St Somewhere, HRGs in orthopaedics were costed and distributed to the host purchaser. HRGs did not form the basis of the contract value, but were used in contract monitoring and for orthopaedic ECR prices. In the West Midlands, HRG prices for 1995/96 showed wide variations, some HRGs having a fourfold variation within the West Midlands Region (*HFMA – West Midlands*, 1996).

The National HFMA Research Committee conducted a survey of purchasers and providers in 1995:

> *'Of the thirteen purchasing authorities responding to the questionnaire, seven indicated that HRGs had played no role at all in the 1995/96 contracting round. For other respondents the use had been very limited. Amongst the acute trusts, however, nine of the fourteen responding to this question indicated that some use had been made by both parties of costed HRG information, although in some cases this was clearly very limited.'*
> *HFMA* (1995)

The contract categories are becoming increasingly complex without standardisation between purchasers. In the West Midlands extended fundholder groups (EFGs) have been introduced for the 1996/97 contracting round. These are to be used for GPFHs, but the previous GPFH treatment classification (plus the further 35 resulting from extension of the fundholding scheme from 1 April 1996) are also priced to provide some continuity (*West Midlands Health Executive*, 1995). To comply with national guidance, the extra-contractual referral prices (ECRs) relate to HRGs.

Two approaches to the development of NHS pricing could be followed. The Executive could seek to refine, monitor and strongly enforce the rules or reduce the need for cost-based pricing rules.

Refine, monitor and enforce the rules

- Establish reasonably homogeneous, standard product groupings to enable meaningful price or cost comparison. The current proliferation of product groupings for pricing purposes exacerbates the situation.
- Make the costing for contracting rules obligatory with very little scope for local discretion.

- Improve openness in costing by requiring information on major areas of resource input. It may be more beneficial to concentrate on providing outcome or output data rather than further disaggregation of costs. Make distribution of the prescribed information compulsory.
- Introduce a strong audit or other compliance monitoring system to ensure adherence to the rules.

Reduce the need for pricing rules

- Take measures to ensure contestability and reduce the need for reliance on cost-based pricing. This will be difficult to achieve because of restrictions on public finance, and duplication of services will lead to inefficiency. However, recent attempts to introduce private finance could improve contestability.
- Employ yardstick competition and selective contracting.
- Accept the reality of the co-operative working relationships between purchasers and providers and that there will often not be a realistic alternative provider (or purchaser). Use yardstick performance to find scope for efficiency savings, including non-financial data, and employ selective contracting for some services (at a level where cost-shifting would be difficult) to ensure that existing service provision is or remains efficient.

11.3 Summary

In the reformed NHS, the internal market separates purchasers and providers of services and attempts to simulate the rigours of a competitive market to produce improved efficiency. In theory, the cost-based pricing rules would imitate the perfectly competitive pricing of neo-classical economics: through the price mechanism and/or openness in costing, providers would be encouraged to be technically efficient and purchasers would use prices to improve allocative efficiency. The premise that cost-based pricing can be adopted to facilitate the achievement of economic efficiency in the NHS internal market is not supported by the research findings.

Acute healthcare services are not conducive to product definition, costing and pricing. The pricing rules relate to the neo-classical single product firm, but provision of healthcare is a diverse service industry with many overhead and indirect costs. To establish meaningful products for contracting requires a reasonable degree of homogeneity, but costing at this level results in few direct costs and the vast majority of costs being apportioned. Accurate costing is therefore complex and subjective. Achieving consistency and comparability for such costs is technically difficult and expensive. Furthermore, strict adherence to full-cost rules is often an unsatisfactory pricing strategy.

Healthcare markets are unlikely to have the features of a competitive market. The emerging NHS internal market is a set of oligopolies and oligopsonies in which inter-organisational bargaining is the central mechanism by which resources are allocated. Rigid full-cost pricing rules are incompatible with the perceptions and incentives operating at individual provider level. The cost-based pricing rules can easily be manipulated at local level and, given the financial management and market incentives, this may frequently arise. The NHS Executive could refine, monitor and strongly enforce the pricing rules and thereby reduce accounting choices. However, such action would be costly and rigid cost accounting methods may actually impede efficient cost management at provider level with no certainty of improvements in overall productive efficiency within the NHS. Consequently, ways to reduce reliance on the pricing rules may be a more attractive alternative.

Appendix 1
Kaiser Foundation Hospitals Fee Schedule

Kaiser Foundation Hospitals, Medical Group & UCLA Medical Center

Exhibit A: fee schedule – Liver Transplantation Servces, 21 February 1991

Liver transplants

(a) Hospital component – adults and pediatrics

The inpatient admission during which a liver transplant is performed:

- For total usual and customary charges less than $160,000, hospitals shall pay $105,000.
- For total usual and customary charges greater than $160,000, and equal to or less than $180,000, hospitals shall pay $120,000.
- For total and usual customary charges greater than $180,000 and less than $200,000, hospitals shall pay $140,000.
- For total and usual customary charges greater than $200,000 and less than $220,000, hospitals shall pay $160,000.
- For total usual and customary charges $220,000 or greater, hospitals shall pay 85% of charges.

+ The above stated 'per case rates' include 4 pre-operative inpatient days. All other additional pre-operative days are reimbursed at a per diem rate of $1,500.
+ The rates include retransplants if performed during the same admission.

+ All usual and customary charges are those in effect as of the commencement date of this agreement.

For the cost of procuring a donor organ from the Regional Organ Procurement Center (ROPA) with ROPA invoice copy, hospitals shall pay 100% of ROPA charges.

For inpatient or outpatient hospital services associated with patient evaluation prior to surgery, or for follow-up care, hospitals shall pay 80% of usual and customary charges in effect at the commencement date of this agreement.

(b) Professional component – adults and pediatrics

(1) Pre-Transplant Services

For services provided during the pre-transplant phase, Medical Group shall compensate for all physician services at 85% of charges. The pre-transplant phase shall be defined as the period of time from referral of the Kaiser member through the fifth day prior to transplantation. Four pre-operative days are included in the transplant admission case rate for both physicians and UCLA Medical Center.

(2) Transplant Services

(a) Adults

For services provided during the the transplant admission for adult cases, Medical Group shall compensate for all physician services at the following case rates:

Medicine and dermatology	$6,515
Psychiatry	$650
Neurology	$150
Surgery:	
surgeon	$13,000
assistants, limit of two per procedure	$2,650 each
Anesthesiology	$4,800
Radiology	$1,600
Pathhology	$800

If a retransplant is necessary during the same admission for adult cases, Medical Group shall compensate for all physician services at the following case rates, in addition to the case rates stated immediately above:

DMPG, medicine and dermatology	$2,215
Psychiatry	$221
Neurology	$50
Surgery:	
surgeon	$8,710
assistants, limit of two per procedure	$1,775 each
Anesthesiology	$4,800
Radiology	$1,600
Pathhology	$800

(b) Pediatrics

For services provided during the transplant admission for pediatric cases, Medical Group shall compensate for all physician services at the following case rates:

Medicine and dermatology	$7,450
Psychiatry	$350
Neurology	$150
Surgery:	
surgeon	$13,000
assistants, limit of two per procedure	$650 each
Anesthesiology	$4,000
Radiology	$1,600
Pathhology	$800

If a retransplant is necessary during the same admission for pediatric cases, Medical Group shall compensate for all physician services at the following rates, in addition to the case rates stated immediately above:

Medicine and dermatology	$2,533
Psychiatry	$150
Neurology	$50
Surgery:	
surgeon	$8,710
assistants, limit of two per procedure	$1,775 each
Anesthesiology	$4,800

Radiology	$1,600
Pathhology	$800

The transplant admission shall include up to four days' care prior to the transplant procedure, and shall terminate upon discharge of the patient from the hospital for the transplant procedure. Additional pre-operative days shall be compensated as part of the pre-transplant phase.

(3) *Post-Transplant Services*

For one year after discharge from the transplant admission, Medical Group shall compensate for all physician services at 85% of charges.

If a retransplant is necessary after discharge from the initial transplant admission, the retransplant will be considered a separate case and the above stated case rates will apply.

Appendix 2: NHS Capital Charges

1. Introduction and objectives

Since its inception the NHS has received separate revenue and capital allocations. Once capital expenditure has been incurred, no further charges arose from the continuing use of the capital asset until the capital charges scheme came into operation on 1 April 1991, introducing charges for the use of capital assets.

The objectives are:

(a) to increase the awareness of health service managers of the costs of capital;
(b) to provide incentives to use capital efficiently;
(c) to ensure that capital charges are fully reflected in the pricing of hospital services, in order to promote fair competition within the NHS and also between the NHS and the private sector.

Capital charges enable contracts with NHS provider units to use prices which reflect the consumption of capital.

2. Scope and definitions

Capital charges are payable on all assets which are owned by the NHS, except for assets acquired by gift (although not forming part of the capital charge, these are depreciated and charged as an expense).

The definition of a capital asset is 'a tangible asset which is capable of being used in an authority's activities for a period which could exceed one year'.

In practice, capital expenditure comprises expenditure over £5,000 (increased from £1,000 on 1 April 1993) on:

(a) acquisition of land and premises;
(b) individual works schemes for the initial provision, extension, improvements, adaptation, upgrading-renewal, replacement or demolition of parts of the estate;
(c) items of equipment, including vehicles;
(d) costs of staff engaged on capital schemes.

3. Valuation of assets and asset lives

The operation of capital charging is dependent upon:

(a) an initial valuation of existing assets
(b) an estimate of the length of life of assets.

Valuation of assets
(a) Land and buildings are valued by district valuers every three years at their current value. Land and buildings held for operational use are valued at their open-market value for existing use; those surplus to requirement are valued at open-market value for alternative use. Values are indexed between the three-year valuations.
(b) Other assets are valued at current cost, which is normally depreciated replacement cost.

Asset lives
Different types of assets have different life expectations, and are therefore depreciated over varying lengths of time. Authorities are required to work to nationally determined standard life expectancies, e.g.:

Vehicles	7 years
Mainframe IT installations	8 years
Furniture	10 years
Engineering installations	5, 10 or 15 years
Main structures	up to 80 years maximum
Land	Permanent: not depreciated

At the inception of the system, assessment was made of the remaining life of all assets. Assessment of building structures was undertaken by the district valuer who determined the remaining life, based on the physical state of the buildings.

In tandem with capital charging, assets are revalued on a current cost basis. The valuation of assets included on an authority's balance sheet will therefore show:

(a) value of assets at current cost replacement value, less
(b) depreciation to date.

4. Capital charges calculations – depreciation and interest

Capital charges consist of two elements – depreciation and interest – and a distinction is made between DMUs and NHS trusts (see (c) below).

(a) *Depreciation*

The depreciation calculation for a financial year is based on the average value of assets during the year. This average is calculated by reference to the actual value of assets at the beginning of each quarter. This means that valuations need to be indexed each quarter and that depreciation is usually charged for complete quarters. There are two methods for calculating depreciation: one for assets subject to periodic revaluation and assessment of remaining life, i.e. buildings, and one for assets with a standard life, i.e. equipment. Both methods are straight-line.

(b) *Interest*

Interest charges are based on the opening value of assets. In order to synchronise the calculation of depreciation and interest, the opening values used are the quarterly ones arrived at for the purposes of the depreciation calculation. The interest rate currently applicable to capital charges is 6 per cent in real terms.

(c) *DMUs v. NHS trusts*

There are important distinctions between DMUs and NHS trusts in respect of capital charge payments (see Figure A2.1 below), although the arrangements have been designed to ensure that there is common treatment of capital costs in the pricing of hospital services.

Figure A2.1: Capital charges

	DMU	NHS trust
Depreciation	Payable to RHA and subsequently allocated to purchasers	Depreciation is retained within the trust. This, together with accumulated surpluses, will be one source of funding for subsequent capital acquisitions. Subject to its external financing limit
Interest	Payable to RHA and subsequently allocated to purchasers	Trusts do not make interest payments but are required to earn a target rate of return (6 per cent) on the current value of their net assets

5. *Impact on resource allocation and pricing for contracts*

Both elements of the capital charge are paid by DMUs to the RHA and form part of the allocation process. In the long term it is intended that this will, as with revenue resources, be in accordance with a resident population-based formula. However, authorities are generally adopting short-term 'protection' arrangements to minimise the disruptive effects of any differences between per capita funding and the charges payable.

The funding flows for capital charges for DMUs are shown in Figure A2.2. In respect of NHS trusts, the arrangements for depreciation and interest outlined above ensures prices are calcuated on a common basis. In order to provide additional finance to DHAs to purchase services from NHS trusts (which is then partly financing trust capital) the DoH transfers resources from capital to revenue which are added to the weighted capital allocation.

Figure A2.2: Funding flows for capital charges to DMUs

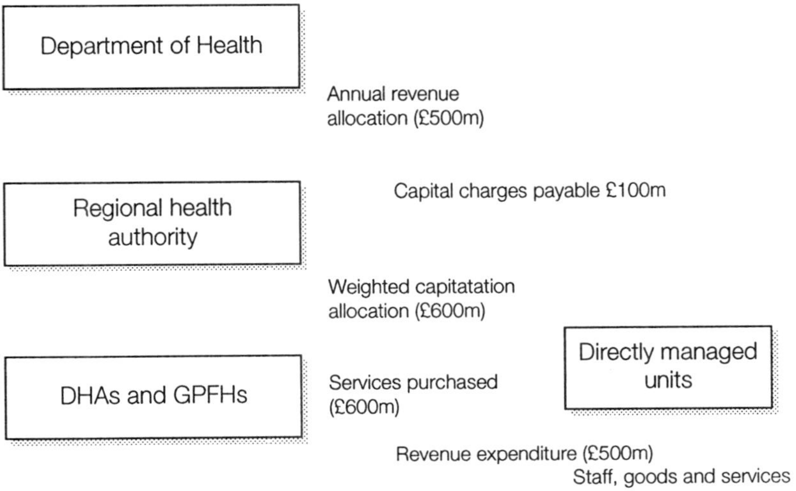

Source: *Introductory Guide to NHS Finance in the UK*,
HFMA/CIPFA (1993)

Bibliography

Appleby, J. (1992), *Financing Health Care in the 1990s*, Open University Press.

Appleby, J., Smith, P., Ranade,W., Little, V. and Robinson, R. (1994), 'Monitoring Managed Competition', in *Evaluating the NHS Reforms*, R. Robinson and J. Le Grand (eds), King's Fund Institute.

Ashford, J. and Cumming, G. (1991), 'Measuring the Costs of Hospital In-patient Care in the NHS', *Health Services Management*, 87 (2): 62-67.

Atkinson, A.A. (1987), *Cost Estimation in Management Accounting – Six Case Studies*, SMA, Toronto.

Audit Commission (1990), *A Short Cut to Better Services: Day Surgery in England and Wales*, HMSO.

Audit Commission (1991), *The Pathology Services: A Management Review*, HMSO.

Audit Commission (1993), *Their Health, your Business: The New Role of the District Health Authority*, HMSO.

Bailey, E.E.(1981), 'Contestability and the Design of Regulatory and Anti-trust Policy', *American Economic Review*, 71 (2): 178-183.

Bailey, E.E., and Baumol, W.J. (1984), 'Deregulation and the Theory of Contestable Markets', *Yale Journal of Regulation*, 1: 111-137.

Bardsley, M., Coles, J. and Jenkins, L. (1989), *DRGs and Health Care*, King Edward's Hospital Fund, London.

Barr, N., Glennerster, H. and Le Grand, J. (1989), *Working for Patients? The Right Approach?*, Welfare State Programme, London School of Economics.

Bartlett, W. (1991), 'Quasi-markets and Contracts: A Markets and Hierarchies Perspective on NHS reform', *Public Money and Management*, Autumn: 53-61.

Bartlett, W. and Le Grand, J. (1992), 'The Impact of NHS Reforms on Hospital Costs', *Studies in Decentralisation and Quasi-markets*, No. 8, School for Advanced Urban Studies, University of Bristol.

Bateson, J.E.G. (1985), 'Perceived Control and the Service Encounter', in *The Service Encounter*, A. Czepiel, M.R. Solomon and C.F. Surprenant (eds) D.C. Heath, Massachusetts.

Baumol, W.J., Panzar, J.C. and Willig, R.D. (1988), *Contestable Markets and the Theory of Industry Structure*, Harcourt Brace Jovanovich, New York.

Baxter, W.T. and Oxenfeldt, A.R. (1968), 'Costing and Pricing: the Cost Accountant versus the Economist', in *Studies in Cost Analysis*, D. Solomons (ed.), Sweet and Maxwell.

Berki, S.E. (1972), *Hospital Economics*, D.C. Heath, Massachusetts.

Berry, L.L. (1981), 'The Employee as Customer', *Journal of Retail Banking*, 3: 33-40.

Bourn, M. and Ezzamel, M. (1986), 'Organizational Culture in Hospitals in the National Health Service', *Financial Accountability and Management*, Autumn, 2 (3): 203-226.

Brimson, J. (1991), *Activity Accounting*, John Wiley, New York.

British Medical Association (BMA) (1989), *Supplementary Report to a Special Conference of Representatives of Local Management Committees* on 27 April 1989, General Medical Services Committee of the British Medical Association, London.

Bromwich, M. and Bhimani, A. (1989), *Management Accounting: Evolution not Revolution*, CIMA.

Brown, S. (1995), 'Costing Initiative may cost NHS over £10m' (news item), *Public Finance*, 27 January, p.6.

Bryan, S. and Beech, R. (1991), 'Cost Information in a Provider Market for Health Care – a note', *Financial Accountability and Management*, 7(2): 84-99.

Burke, C. and Goddard, A. (1990), 'Internal Markets – the Road to Inefficiency', *Public Administration*, 68 Autumn: 389-396.

Butler, J. (1992), *Patients, Policies and Politics*, Open University Press.

Buxton, M., Packwood,T., and Keen, J. (1989), *Resource Management: Process and Progress*, Health Economics Research Group, Brunel University.

Buxton, M., Packwood,T., and Keen, J. (1991), *Final Report of the Brunel University Evaluation of Resource Management*, Brunel University.

Carter, G. and Ginsburg, P. (1985), *The Medicare Case-mix Index Increase: Medical Practice Changes, Ageing and DRG Creep*, R-3292-HCFA, Rand Corporation, Santa Monica.

Central Consultants and Specialists Committee (1989), *Resource Management Initiative: an Evaluation of the Six Experimental Sites*, BMA, London.

Chan, Y-C., L. (1993), 'Improving Hospital Cost Accounting with Activity Based Costing', *Health Care Management Review*, 18 (1): 71-77, Aspen Publishers Inc.

Chandler, A.D. (1977), *The Visible Hand: the Managerial Revolution in American Business*, Harvard University Press.

CIMA (1993), *Management Accounting Guides for the NHS: Activity Based Costing*, CIMA.

CIPFA (1990), *Health Database 1990*, CIPFA.

CIPFA (1992), *Health Database 1992 Volume 1, Financial Overview*, CIPFA.

Clarke, J.M. (1923), *Studies in the Economics of Overhead Costs*, University of Chicago Press.

Coase, R. (1937), 'The Nature of the Firm', *Economica,* 4: 386-405.

Cooper, R. (1990), 'Cost Classification in Unit-Based and Activity-Based Manufacturing Cost Systems', *Journal of Cost Management*, 4 (3), 4-14.

Cooper, R. and Kaplan, R.S. (1988), 'Measure Costs Right: Make the Right Decisions', *Harvard Business Review*, September–October 1988.

Cooper, R. and Kaplan, R.S. (1992), 'Activity Based Systems: Measure the Costs of Resource Usage', *Accounting Horizons*, September: 1-13.

Counte, M.A. and Glandon, G.L. (1988), 'Managerial Innovation in the Hospital: An Analysis of the Diffusion of Hospital Cost Accounting Systems', *Hospital and Health Services Administration*, Fall 33 (3): 371-84.

Culyer, A.J. and Posnett, J. (1990), 'Hospital Behaviour and Competition', in *Competition in Health Care*, Culyer et al. (ed.), Macmillan.

Dawson, D. (1994), *Costs and Prices in the Internal Market: Market vs the NHS Management Executive Guidelines*, Discussion Paper 115, Centre for Health Economics, University of York.

Department of Health (1989a), *Working for Patients*, HMSO.

Department of Health (1989b), Self governing hospitals, *Working for Patients,* Working Paper No. 1, HMSO.

Department of Health (1989c), Funding and contracts for hospital services, *Working for Patients,* Working Paper No. 2, HMSO.

Department of Health (1989d), Practice budgets for General Medical Practitioners, *Working for Patients,* Working Paper No. 3, HMSO.

Department of Health (1989e), Medical Audit, *Working for Patients,* Working Paper No. 6, HMSO.

Department of Health (1989f), EL(89) MB/171, *Contracts for Health Services: Pricing and 'Openness' – A Discussion Document*, HMSO.

Department of Health (1990), *Contracts for Health Services: Operating Contracts*, HMSO.

DHSS (1984), *Steering Group on Health Service Information* (Chairman: Mrs E. Korner), Sixth Report to the Secretary of State, HMSO.

DHSS (1986) *Health Service Management – Resource Management (Management Budgeting) in Health Authorities*, Health Notice, HN(86)34.

Donaldson, C. and Gerard, K. (1993), *Economics of Health Care Financing – The Visible Hand*, Macmillan.

Drury, C. (1992), *Management and Cost Accounting*, Chapman & Hall.

Ellwood, S. (1992), *Cost Methods for NHS Healthcare Contracts*, CIMA.

Enthoven, A. C. (1985), *Reflections on the Management of the National Health Service*, Nuffield Provincial Hospitals Trust.

Ferguson, B. and Posnett, J. (1990), *Pricing and Openness in Contracts for Healthcare Services*, Occasional Paper 11, Centre for Health Economics, University of York.

Fitzgerald, L., Johnston, R., Brignall, S., Silvestro, R. and Voss, C. (1991), *Performance Measurement in Service Industries*, CIMA.

Fisk, R.P. and Freshley, C. (1981), 'Marketing Applications of Hospital Laboratory Services', *Journal of Health Care Marketing*, 1, 2: 33-39.

Glennerster, H., Matsaganis, M. and Owens, P. (1992), *A Foothold for Fundholding*, Research Report 12, King's Fund Institute.

Govindarajan, V. and Anthony, R. (1983), 'How Firms Use Cost Data in Pricing Decisions', *Management Accounting*, July: 30-36.

Griffiths, R. (1983), *NHS Management Inquiry (The Griffiths Report)*, DHSS.

Griffiths, R. (1988), *Community Care: Agenda for Action*, HMSO.

Guterman, S. and Dobson, A. (1986), 'Impact of the Medicare Prospective Payment System for Hospitals', *Health Care Financing Review*, 7: 97-114.

Ham, C., Robinson, R. and Benzeval, M. (1990), *Health Check – Health Care Reforms in an International Context*, King's Fund Institute.

Hayek, F.A. (1984), *1980s Unemployment and the Union*, Hobert Paper 87, Second Edition, IEA.

HFMA Massachusetts Chapter USA (1991), *Cost Accounting, Budgeting and Decision Support Practices in Massachusetts' Hospitals* (unpublished survey).

HFMA/ CIPFA (1992), *Guide to Good Practice – Costing: Activity Based Costing*, CIPFA.

HFMA/ CIPFA (1993), *Introductory Guide to NHS Finance in the UK*, HFMA/ CIPFA.

HFMA National Research Committee Report (1995), *The Regulatory Framework and Market Environment.*

HFMA West Midlands Research Group (1994), *Costing and Pricing Contracts 1994/95 (acute services)*, unpublished survey.

HFMA West Midlands Research Group (1996), *HRG Costing and Pricing 1995/96*, unpublished survey.

Higgins, W. (1991), 'Myths of Competitive Reform', *Healthcare Management Review*, 16 (1): 65-72.

Hillman, R.L. and Nix, G.R. (1983), *DHSS-Funded Research into Specialty Costing 1980–1982*, DHSS.

Hollingsworth, J and Hollingsworth, E. (1987), *Controversy about American Hospitals: Funding Ownership and Performance*, American Enterprise Institute.

Howard, T.P. (1979), A Comparison of Two Methods of Cost Finding, *Proceedings of the Southwestern Regional Meeting*, American Accounting Association.

Johnson, H.T. (1988), 'Activity Based Information: A Blueprint for World Class Management Accounting', *Management Accounting* (USA), June: 23-30.

Joskow, P.L. (1983), 'Reimbursement Policy, Cost Containment and Non-price Competition', *Journal of Health Economics*, 2: 167-174.

Jowell, R. (1988), *British Social Attitudes: the 5th Report*, Gower.

Kay, J. and Vickers, J. (1990), 'Regulatory Reform', in *Deregulation or Reregulation? Regulatory Reform in Europe and the United States*, G.Majone (ed.), Pinter.

King, M., Lapsley, I., Mitchell, F. and Moyes, J. (1994), *Activity Based Costing in Hospitals – A Case Study Investigation*, CIMA.

Lapsley, I. (1993), 'Markets, Hierarchies and the Regulation of the National Health Service', *Accounting and Business Research*, 23 (91): 384-94.

Le Grand, J. (1991), 'Quasi-markets and Social Policy', *The Economic Journal*, 101 (408), September: 1256-1267.

Le Grand, J. (1994), 'Quasi-markets and Social Policy', in *Policy and Change*, R. Smith and J. Raistrick (eds), School for Advanced Urban Studies, University of Bristol.

Le Grand, J. and Bartlett, W. (1993), *Quasi-markets and Social Policy*, Macmillan.

Le Grand, J. and Robinson, R. (1984), *The Economics of Social Problems – The Market Versus the State*, Macmillan.

Liebenstein, H. (1966), 'Allocative Efficiency vs X-efficiency', *American Economic Review*, 56.

Luft, H. (1986), 'The Role of Specialised Services in Competition among Hospitals', *Inquiry*, 23: 83-94.

McAlister, D. (1994), 'Putting Health Economics into Quality', *Public Money and Management*, 14 (2): 15-22.

McFadden, D.W. (1990), 'The Legacy of the $7 Aspirin', *Management Accounting* (USA): 38-41.

McGuire, A., Henderson, J. and Mooney, G. (1988), *The Economics of Health Care*, Routledge & Kegan Paul.

MacKerrell, D.K.D. (1993), 'Contract Pricing: A Management Opportunity', in *Managing the Internal Market*, I.Tilley, (ed.), Paul Chapman.

Matsaganis, M. and Glennerster, H. (1994), 'Cream-skimming and Fundholding', in *Quasi-Markets and the Welfare State*, W. Bartlett, C. Propper, D. Wilson and J. Le Grand (eds), School for Advanced Urban Studies, University of Bristol.

Maxwell, R.J. (1988), 'Financing Healthcare: Lessons from Abroad', *British Medical Journal*, 296: 1423-6.

Mayston, D. (1990), 'NHS Resourcing: A Financial and Economic Analysis', in *Competition in Health Care*, A.J. Culyer, A.K. Maynard and J.W. Posnett (eds), Macmillan.

Melnick, G.A. and Zwanziger, J. (1988), 'Hospital Behavior under Competition and Cost Containment Policies: the California Experience 1980 to 1985', *Journal of the American Medical Association*, 260: 2669- 2675.

Mellet, H., Marriot, N. and Harries, S. (1993), *Financial Management in the NHS: A Manager's Handbook*, Chapman & Hall.

Mohr, L.B. (1985), 'The Reliability of the Case Study as a Source of Information', in *Advances in Information Processing in Organizations*, R. Coulam and R. Smith (eds), vol. 2, JAI Press.

Mooney, G. (1992), *Economics, Medicine and Health Care*, Harvester Wheatsheaf.

NAHAT (1991), *A Review of Capital Charges in the NHS: Cutting through the Confusion*, NAHAT.

NAHAT (1993), *Monitoring the White Paper: Managed Competition*, NAHAT.

National Audit Office (1987), *Use of Operating Theatres in the National Health Service*, HMSO.

NHS Management Board (1989), *Case-mix Management System: Core Specification.*

NHSME (1990a), *Costing and Pricing Contracts: Cost Allocation Principles.*

NHSME (1990b), *Costing and Pricing Contracts*, EL(90)173.

NHSME (1990c), *Costing and Pricing Contracts, Experience of the Cost Demonstration Sites.*

NHSME (1991), *Working for Patients: Starting Specifications, A DHA Project Paper*, Department of Health.

NHSME (1992), FDL(92)70.

NHSME (1993a), *Costing for Contracting*, EL(93)26 – 6 April.

NHSME (1993b), *Costing for Contracting*, EL(93)62 – 21 July.

NHSME (1993c), *Costing for Contracting Manual*, issued August 1993.

NHSME (1993d), *Costing for Contracting – The 1994/95 Contracting Round*, FDL(93)59.

NHS Executive (1994a), *Comparative Cost Data: The Use of HRGs to Inform the Contracting Process*, EL(94)51.

NHS Executive (1994b), Letter dated 8 March from Executive Director M. Biddle.

Newhouse, J.P. and Byrne, D.J., (1988), 'Did Medicare's Prospective Payment System Cause Length of Stay to Fall?', *Journal of Health Economics*, 7: 413-416.

OECD (1989), *Health Data File*, Directorate of Social Affairs, Manpower and Education, OECD.

Okun, A. (1981), *Prices and Quantities: A Macroeconomic Analysis*, Brookings Institution.

Orloff, T.M., Littell, C.L., Clune, C., Klingman, D. and Preston, B. (1990), 'Hospital Cost Accounting: Who's doing what and why', *Health Care Management Review*, 15 (4): 73-78.

Ouchi, W.G. (1993), 'Markets, Bureaucracies and Clans', in *Markets, Hierarchies and Networks – the coordination of social life*, G. Thompson, J. Frances, R. Levacic and J. Mitchell (eds), Sage.

Packwood, T., Buxton, M. and Keen, J. (1991), *Hospitals in Transition*, Open University Press.

Panzar, J.C. and Willig, R.D. (1975), *Economies of Scale and Economies of Scope in Multi-output Production*, Bell Laboratories Economic Discussion Paper No. 33.

Panzar, J.C. and Willig, R.D. (1977), 'Economies of Scale in Multi-output Production', *Quarterly Journal of Economics*, 91: 481-494.

Panzar, J.C. and Willig, R.D. (1979), *Economies of Scope, Product-specific Economies of Scale and the Multiproduct Competitive Firm*, Bell Laboratories Economic Discussion Paper No. 152.

Perrin, J. (1988), *Resource Management in the NHS*, Chapman & Hall.

Piper, J. and Walley, P. (1990), 'Testing ABC Logic', *Management Accounting* (UK), September.

Piper, J. and Walley, P. (1991), 'ABC Relevance Not Found', *Management Accounting* (UK), March.

Propper, C., Bartlett, W., Wilson, D. and Le Grand, J. (1994), *Quasi-markets in the Welfare State*, School for Advanced Urban Studies, University of Bristol.

Roberts, H. (1990), *Outcome and Performance in Health Care*, Public Finance Foundation.

Robinson, J. (1987), 'Market and Regulatory Influences on the Availability of Coronary Angioplasty and Bypass Surgery in US Hospitals', *New England Journal of Medicine*, 317: 85-90.

Robinson, J. and Luft, H. (1985), 'Competition and the Cost of Hospital Care', *Journal of the American Medical Association*, 257 (23): 3241-5.

Robinson, R. (1988), *Efficiency and the NHS: A Case for Internal Markets?* IEA Health Unit.

Robinson R. (1990), *Competition and Health Care: a comparative analysis of UK plans and US experience*, Research Report No. 6, King's Fund Institute.

Robinson, R. (1991), 'Who's Playing Monopoly', *Health Service Journal*, 28 March.

Robinson, R. (1994), 'Hospitals in the Market', in *Information Management in Health Services*, J. Keen (ed.), Open University Press.

Robinson, R. and Le Grand, J. (1994), *Evaluating the NHS Reforms*, King's Fund Institute.

Rosko, M.D. and Broyles, R.W. (1987), 'Short Term Responses of Hospitals to the DRG Prospective Pricing Mechanism in New Jersey', *Medical Care*, 25: 88-99.

Ryan, R., Scapens, R.W. and Theobald, M. (1992), *Research Method and Methodology in Finance and Accounting*, Academic Press.

Sanderson, H.F., Storey, A., Morris, D., McNay, R.A., Robson, M.P. and Loeb, J. (1989), 'Evaluation of Diagnoses-Related Groups in the National Health Service', *Community Medicine,* 11 (4): 269-278.

Schimmel, V.E., Alley, C. and Mullaney-Heath, A. (1987), 'Measuring Costs: Product Line Accounting versus Ratio of Cost to Charges', *Top Health Care Finance*, 13 (4): 76-86.

Sizer, J. (1989), *An Insight into Management Accounting*, Penguin.

Sloan, F.A., Morrissey, M.A. and Valvona, J. (1983), 'Medicare Prospective Payment and the Use of Medical Technologies in Hospitals', *Medical Care*, 26: 837-853.

Smith, A. (1976), *An Inquiry into the Nature and Causes of the Wealth of Nations* (first published 1776), Clarendon Press.

Stoline, A. and Weiner, J.P. (1988), *The New Medical Market Place: A Physician's Guide to the Healthcare Revolution*, Johns Hopkins University Press.

Sutcliffe, C. (1991), 'Aggregation and Reciprocal Service Cost Allocation', *Journal of Business Finance and Accounting*, 18 (5): 721-733.

Suver, J.D., Neumann, B.R. and Boles, K.E. (1992), *Management Accounting for Healthcare Organizations*, Pluribus Press Inc. and HFMA.

Thompson, G. (1993), 'Comparison between Models', in *Markets, Hierarchies and Networks – the coordination of social life*, G. Thompson, J. Frances, R. Levacic and J. Mitchell (eds), Sage.

Vita, M.G. (1990), 'Exploring Hospital Production Relationships with Flexible Function Forms', *Journal of Health Economics*, 9 (1): 1-22.

Wagstaff, A. (1989), 'Econometric Studies in Health Economics: A Survey of the British Literature', *Journal of Health Economics*, 8: 1-51.

Weiner, J. and Ferris, P. (1990), *GP Budget Holding in the UK: Lessons from America*, Research Report 7, King's Fund Institute.

West Midlands Health Executive (1995), *1996/97 GP Fundholding Budget Setting and Pricing Policy*.

Williamson, O.E. (1971), 'Managerial Discretion, Organization Form, and the Multi-division Hypothesis', in *The Corporate Economy*, R. Marris and A. Wood (eds), Harvard University Press.

Williamson, O.E. (1975), *Markets and Hierarchies: Analysis and Antitrust Implications*, Free Press.

Wise, J. (1992), *Hospital Cost Accounting in the United States*, CIPFA.

Yates, J. (1987), *Why Are We Waiting? An Analysis of Hospital Waiting Lists*, Oxford University Press.